CW00434664

Developing High Performance Teams

Chartered Management Institute Open Learning Programme

OTHER BOOKS WITHIN THIS SERIES

DEVELOPING HIGH PERFORMANCE TEAMS

Second edition

Revised by: Corinne Leech

Series Editor: Kate Williams

Pergamon
Flexible
Learning

chartered
management
institute

ELSEVIER

AMSTERDAM • BOSTON • HEIDELBERG • LONDON • OXFORD • NEW YORK • PARIS
• SAN DIEGO • SAN FRANCISCO • SINGAPORE • SYDNEY • TOKYO

Elsevier
Linacre House, Jordan Hill, Oxford OX2 8DP
200 Wheeler Road, Burlington, MA 01803

First published in 1997
Second edition 2004

Copyright © Chartered Management Institute, 1997. All rights reserved
Copyright © Elsevier Limited, 2004. All rights reserved

No part of this publication may be reproduced in any material form (including
photocopying or storing in any medium by electronic means and whether or not
transiently or incidentally to some other use of this publication) without the
written permission of the copyright holder except in accordance with the provisions
of the Copyright, Designs and Patents Act 1988 or under the terms of a licence
issued by the Copyright Licensing Agency Ltd, 90 Tottenham Court Road,
London, England W1T 4LP. Applications for the copyright holder's written
permission to reproduce any part of this publication should be addressed to the
publishers

Permissions may be sought directly from Elsevier's Science and Technology
Rights Department in Oxford, UK: phone: (+44) (0) 1865 843830; fax: (+44) (0)
1865 853333; e-mail: permissions@elsevier.co.uk. You may also complete your
request on-line via the Elsevier homepage (http://www.elsevier.com), by selecting 'Customer Support' and then 'Obtaining Permissions'

British Library Cataloguing in Publication Data
A catalogue record for this book is available from the British Library

ISBN 0 7506 64207

For information on all Elsevier publications visit our website at
http://books.elsevier.com

Revised by: Corinne Leech
Editor: Kate Williams
Based on previous material in the Chartered Management Institute Opening
Learning Programme, 1997; Series Editor: Gareth Lewis.

Typeset by Charon Tec Pvt. Ltd, Chennai, India
Printed and bound in Italy

Contents

Series overview

The Chartered Management Institute Flexible Learning Programme is a series of workbooks prepared by the Chartered Management Institute and Elsevier for managers seeking to develop themselves.

Comprising ten open learning workbooks, the programme covers the best of modern management theory and practice. Each workbook provides a range of frameworks and techniques to improve your effectiveness as a manager, thus helping you acquire the knowledge and skill to make you fully competent in your role.

Each workbook is written by an experienced management writer and covers an important management topic or theme. The activities both reinforce learning and help to relate the generic ideas to your individual work context. While coverage of each topic is fully comprehensive, additional reading suggestions and reference sources are given for those who wish to study to a greater depth.

Designed to be practical, stimulating and challenging, the aim of the workbooks is to improve performance at work by benefiting you and your organization. This practical focus is at the heart of the competence-based approach that has been adopted by the programme.

Introduction

The development of people adds value to any organization. People who have regular, consistent opportunities to update their skills and knowledge, who are empowered to use their initiative, think for themselves and take responsibility for their actions will bring benefits. Being actively supported to develop by their line manager feeds people's need to feel valued, respected and appreciated.

There are two main types of development:

- career development
- personal development.

Career development is related to your 'job path'; the roles you take on in your working life. Personal development is about the way you evolve as a person. Inevitably the two are inextricably linked as you bring the behaviours and skills you develop as a person to your job role. As a manager you are likely to focus on the career development of your team whilst recognizing the value that any form of personal development can bring to the work situation.

The importance of development is highlighted by John Adair[1] in his ideas on action-centred leadership. Adair maintains that effective leaders meet three interlocking needs of teams (Figure I.1):

Figure I.1

- The need to achieve a common task
- The need to maintain good relationships within the team
- The needs of individual members of a team.

Effective managers must focus on meeting all three needs if they are to create a high performing team. An important method of ensuring individual needs are met is by making sure each member of the team has development opportunities.

This workbook focuses on your role in developing your team members. It looks at the importance of understanding yourself, your team members and the organization so that development opportunities can be tailored accordingly. It also focuses on the practicalities of analysing development needs and using the following development techniques:

- Training session
- Coaching
- Delegating
- Mentoring.

Objectives

By the end of the workbook you will be better able to:

- recognize your preferred style of leadership
- identify characteristics of team members which are likely to affect how they can maximize the benefits of development opportunities
- review how you identify development needs within your team
- plan, deliver and evaluate a training event
- coach team members to develop their skills
- use delegation as a method of developing members of your team
- recognize the benefits and practicalities of introducing a mentoring programme into an organization.

Reference

1   Adair J. *Action-Centred Leadership*, Gower (1979)

Section 1 Creating an environment for development

Introduction

It is often convenient for managers to see the training department as being responsible for the development of people. However, the most effective development often takes place in the workplace when the line manager is fully involved in:

- identifying the development needs
- supporting the development
- checking that the skills and knowledge have been transferred to the workplace.

The training department can supply expertise to the process and also source training courses. However, responsibility for development must stay with the line manager and team member.

Before taking on the role of developing members of your team you need to understand:

1. how you, as the leader of your team, are perceived by team members
2. something about what your team members will be bringing to any development exercise.

Therefore this section introduces some of the management models and concepts which will give you a greater understanding of the interactions between you and your team members. You can then use this knowledge to tailor the range of development techniques which we explore in later sections.

Understanding your leadership style

Your management style will have a big impact on the culture you create in your team and, in turn, the attitude towards development. A great deal of work has been done on the classification and categorization of different kinds of leadership. We look at:

- situational leadership
- autocratic to democratic leadership.

We'll review each one and then consider the impact it has on encouraging development within a team.

SITUATIONAL LEADERSHIP

Paul Hersey[1] and Ken Blanchard identified four main styles of leadership:

Directing style

A manager using a directing style will be decisive and give instructions as to how things should be done. They expect people to follow orders, carry out tasks in accordance with their requirements and see things their way. They may find it difficult to let go and let people get on with things in their own way.

Positive aspects

- Particularly helpful for new and inexperienced team members.
- People have the information they need to perform their job to the standard required (assuming the manager gives clear instructions and explanations).
- People know what they have to do, how they have to do it and what will happen if they don't.
- There is a measure of safety and security as people know where they stand.

Negative aspects

- People who are not allowed to use their initiative, individuality or creativity quickly become frustrated, bored or rebellious.
- When a manager makes decisions without consultation people do not have ownership of anything. As a result, morale and motivation are likely to dip, often quite dramatically.
- The directive manager, left unchecked, can be domineering and autocratic.

Coaching style

Using this style the manager is good at involving people in the decision-making process and is willing to take the time and trouble to help people solve problems. They may become too involved with discussions about people's problems.

Positive aspects

- Team members are given many opportunities to talk things through.
- Team members can benefit from adopting a joint problem-solving approach with their manager.
- Team members appreciate the fact that their manager is willing to work alongside them.

Negative aspects

- Manager may step in and make decisions which team members could quite easily make on their own.
- Manager may have a tendency to use talking as a substitute for action.

Supporting style

This style allows people to take responsibility but they know that the manager is there to give support when needed. The manager is willing to listen and offer wholehearted support.

Positive aspects

- Team members are given challenging tasks and projects which stretch them.
- Team feels encouraged and supported and have the confidence to be open and honest.

Negative aspects

- Manager may have difficulty finding time for own work in their desire to be approachable and available.
- Resistance to give orders may mean that less experienced members of the team are not sure of their role and responsibilities.

Delegating style

Managers are good at giving people the freedom to develop their own ideas and take ownership of major tasks and projects. They are willing to let go and trust team members to do a good job on their own.

Positive aspects

- The team develops quickly because they have to use their initiative and often find they are capable of more than they originally thought.
- Team members feel trusted and empowered.

Negative aspects

- Manager may have a tendency to just 'walk away' and let team get on with it.
- Unavailability may seem like abdication of responsibility.
- Even highly experienced team members may experience problems and may be reluctant to discuss them with the manager.

As a manager you are likely to have a preferred style; one that you feel most comfortable using. However, you should be able to adapt your style to the situation – hence the term situational leadership. It involves recognizing that your team will need you to take on the different styles under different circumstances and adapting accordingly. Some examples of appropriate circumstances for each of these leadership styles include the following.

Directing style

- when dealing with new, uncertain or inexperienced team members who need to be told what to do
- when team members are getting confused or overloaded with work
- when people require a manager's specialist skills and experience.

Coaching style

- when dealing with people who are reasonably competent but who need additional help with specific tasks or skills
- when team members need help with problem solving
- when team members are trying out new ideas and approaches
- when new systems or processes are being introduced and the team needs the manager to work alongside them.

Supporting style

- when team members are really performing but still need to know that the manager is available
- when a manager is prepared to develop the team by involving everyone in the decision-making process.

Delegating style

- when team members are highly experienced and competent
- when people's confidence and skills can be developed through delegating
- when a manager wants to demonstrate that individual team members or the whole team have complete trust.

ACTIVITY 1

Identify at least one occasion when you have used the different styles of leadership identified by Blanchard and Hersey.

Style of leadership	Occasion when you used the style to develop a member of your team
Directive style	
Coaching style	
Supporting style	
Delegating style	

What is your preferred style of leadership using this model?

Circumstances in the workplace often make it likely that you will *either* more frequently use a directive/coaching approach *or* a supporting/delegating approach to develop people. However, you should be able to select an approach because it's the best option given the circumstances; not because you feel more comfortable with it.

AUTOCRATIC TO DEMOCRATIC LEADERSHIP

The leadership model developed by Tannenbaum and Schmidt[2] is a continuum with autocratic at one end and democratic at the other and focuses on how decisions are made within a team.

Autocratic					Democratic
1	2	3	4	5	6
Manager takes decision alone, without any consultation.	Manager takes decision alone but 'sells' benefits to team members.	Manager presents ideas for discussion and **pretends** to consult (already has chosen preferred option).	Manager presents ideas for discussion and genuinely consults.	Manager presents ideas and asks team to decide – subject to certain limits and boundaries.	Manager joins the team in decision-making process.

ACTIVITY 2

What is your preferred style on the autocratic–democratic decision-making continuum?

Identify an occasion when you used a completely autocratic style of decision-making.

Identify an occasion when you used a completely democratic style of decision-making.

FEEDBACK

Again, it is important to note that the most appropriate decision-making style will depend on many factors including the people involved, the issue, the circumstances, the timing and the culture of the organization. Effective managers are flexible and adapt and respond to the circumstances of the moment. In your role in developing members of team you need to focus on selecting the appropriate style to complement the chosen development method. For example an autocratic approach to decision-making would match a directive style of leadership and would be most appropriate to use when members of your team need to be told clearly what to do.

Understanding your team

The rich variety of human nature is what makes relationships – at home and at work – so diverse, interesting, stimulating and, of course, challenging. Every individual has his or her own:

- likes and dislikes
- attitude and approaches
- values and beliefs
- speed of thought and action
- level of intelligence and creativity
- level of need for social interaction
- desire for risk and challenge, or – desire for stability and tranquility.

So in a team of three people the result could be similar to that shown in Figure 1.1.

Lynn	Mike	Sanjeet
■ Likes the countryside and enjoys a very quiet social life, preferring to spend time at home reading and sewing. Abhors television.	■ Likes sport and socializing with friends. Subscriber to Sky television and cheerfully admits he is addicted to watching late-night movies. Regular churchgoer.	■ Likes pubs and clubs and a varied and frenetic social life.
■ Lives with her partner of 10 years.	■ Married, two children.	■ Single, lives alone, enjoys a variety of relationships while steering clear of commitment to any one person.
■ Practising Buddhist.	■ Committed Christian.	■ Absolute atheist.

Figure 1.1

They all have very different attitudes and approaches towards life. It doesn't mean that one person is right, making the other two wrong. It just means they are *different*. The one factor which people have in common is that **they are all different**. One of the keys to building a high performance team is to recognize and accept these differences, and to make them work for the good of the team. We focus on the following three areas where team members will be different:

- Competence and commitment
- Team roles
- Learning styles.

COMPETENCE AND COMMITMENT

The style of leadership you use when developing individual members of your team will depend on:

- their level of competence
- their commitment level.

Two questions need to be asked:

- How competent is this person? How good are they at their job? How much direction do they need?
- How committed is this person? To what extent do they work willingly and well? How much support and encouragement do they need?

In terms of competence and commitment, most team members will fit into one of the four main categories as shown in Figure 1.2.

CATEGORY 1	**CATEGORY 2**
Low competence	**Some competence**
Inexperienced; needs additional training and development opportunities; needs updating on skills or knowledge; needs supervision.	Some experience; additional training and development opportunities would be useful and helpful; needs some supervision.
High commitment	**Low commitment**
Enthusiastic, confident, hard-working, eager to learn and develop, highly motivated.	Not particularly enthusiastic or confident or hard-working or eager to learn and develop; not particularly motivated.
CATEGORY 3	**CATEGORY 4**
High competence	**High competence**
Highly skilled, competent and experienced; knows precisely what they are supposed to do and how to do it; capable and competent; can work unsupervised.	Highly skilled, competent and experienced; knows precisely what they are supposed to do and how to do it; capable and competent; can work unsupervised.
Variable commitment	**High commitment**
Sometimes enthusiastic, confident, hard-working, eager to learn and develop, highly motivated – and sometimes not.	Always enthusiastic, confident, hard-working, eager to learn and develop, highly motivated.

Figure 1.2   The four categories of competence and commitment

This can be shown visually (see Figure 1.3).

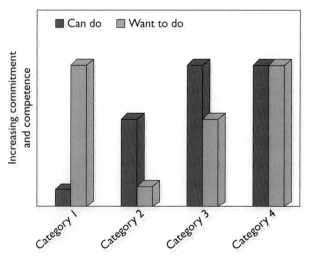

Figure 1.3   The four states of competence and motivation

ACTIVITY 3

Consider the people in your team. Enter their names in the left hand column and tick the appropriate box.

(To preserve confidentiality, you may prefer to use a separate piece of paper)

Name	Category 1 Low competence/ High commitment	Category 2 Some competence/ Low commitment	Category 3 High competence/ Variable commitment	Category 4 High competence/ High commitment

FEEDBACK

People who fall into:

- **category 1** tend to respond best to lots of direction. Their motivation is high but they need clear direction and some supervision to compensate for their lack of skills and knowledge.
- **category 2** tend to respond best to a coaching style. They need some direction and supervision, plus regular praise and encouragement to build motivation.
- **category 3** tend to respond best to a supporting style. They know what they are doing, so need little supervision, but they do need a fair amount of encouragement.
- **category 4** tend to respond best to a delegating style. Even so, don't make the mistake of always leaving category 4 people to just get on with it. They need feedback and encouragement just as much as anyone else.

THE ROLES PEOPLE PLAY IN TEAMS

It is always useful to be able to recognize the roles people play in teams. People, at home and at work, function in different ways. Some are extrovert and need people, some are introvert and prefer their own company. Some are neat, tidy and highly organized, while others are careless, slapdash and highly disorganized. It doesn't mean that one is better than the other, although we often approve of those who are more like us, and disapprove of those who are not like us.

The Cambridge psychologist, Meredith Belbin, has identified eight different roles which people play when working in a team situation. The term *team role* describes the way in which an individual will operate and function within a team and encompasses the way he or she:

- relates to the other team members
- communicates with the other team members
- contributes to the team.

As a manager it is helpful to be able to:

1 **understand the differences between the individual people on the team**   (what is this person like? how do they prefer to operate? what does he or she do best?)
2 **understand the differences between the team roles**   (what strengths and weaknesses does this role bring to the team? what does this team role contribute to the team?)
3 **allow people to operate in their own, natural team role strengths**. This is about allowing people to be themselves and to contribute to the team in the way that naturally suits them best. This is really fitting square pegs into square holes, and round pegs into round holes. When the *match* and *fit* are right, people will feel comfortable and at ease. They will feel they are making a genuine contribution to the team because their input will be **suited to their temperament and capabilities.**

Belbin's eight team roles are described below.

The Plant

Someone who fits the description of Plant is:

- **an ideas person**   Their ideas are usually original, radical, imaginative and *different,* and they have a strong intellectual grasp of concepts and they like to tackle and solve complex, difficult problems.
- **an unorthodox person**   They prefer to work independently (rather than run with the herd), and they have an unconventional approach to life and

relationships. If they are caught up in a knotty problem a Plant will appear at a board meeting wearing laddered tights or the remains of last night's supper on their tie. Appearances and protocols are unimportant – the intellectual challenge is the thing.

- their greatest contribution to the team is original thought, the ability to generate new and interesting ideas, and to solve complex problems
- their greatest failings are:
  - their ability (and desire) to live 'up in the clouds'
  - their inability to attend to detail (they prefer the big picture)
  - their sensitivity; they don't like criticism and have difficulty accepting praise
  - their inability to communicate easily with people who are not as bright or as unconventional as they are.

The Resource Investigator

Someone who fits the description of Resource Investigator is:

- **a 'people' person** They need the stimulation of meeting and talking to others. They enjoy being out and about, networking with people away from the office, or communicating on the phone. They love to trawl for new ideas, or take an existing concept and expand it into something new and exciting.
- they are positive and optimistic, relaxed and gregarious, usually well liked and popular.
- **a diplomatic person** They are skilled negotiators who enjoy thinking on their feet and relish the challenge of working out a favourable deal.
- their greatest contribution to the team is energy, optimism and enthusiasm, which can help to motivate the other team members when the outlook is bleak and stormy.
- their greatest failings are:
  - their lack of stamina. They can get very enthusiastic about something new, but, if unsupported by the rest of the team, they will quickly lose heart and move on to a better, more interesting, more exciting idea
  - their need for contact with people and for positive feedback
  - their tendency to be over optimistic: 'Hey, it'll be all right on the night!'

The Co-ordinator

Someone who fits the description of Co-ordinator is:

- **a controlled and calm person** They have the ability to recognize other people's strengths and capabilities and then co-ordinate those elements for the good of the team.
- **a skilled communicator** They are adept at drawing out from each team member their views and opinions, and then summarizing and articulating the temperature and mood of the team.

- **a strong and steady person**   They are calm and unflappable and often have a natural air of authority. When a crisis looms and a cool head is needed, the Coordinator is the person who can pull the team together.
- **a focused person**   No matter what happens, they will help to keep the team focused on the tasks and activities which will lead towards achieving the desired outcome.
- their greatest contribution to the team is their ability to unify the team and remind the team of the goals and objectives for which everyone is working so hard.
- their greatest failings are:
  - their lack of creativity, zing and charisma.

The Shaper

Someone who fits the description of Shaper is:

- **a pushy person**   They are extrovert, energetic, restless and, often, neurotic. They are results orientated, and will push and push to make things happen. They drive themselves hard – and drive everyone else on the team, too.
- **an impulsive person**   They see something that needs to be done, and they will plunge straight in and do it – sometimes forgetting that consultation is part of the diplomatic process.
- **a thick-skinned person**   They are able to work well in the midst of dissension and politically-charged atmospheres because they will just get on with their job, regardless of what is happening around them. Their ability to bulldoze their way through situations can often upset gentler, more sensitive team members.
- their greatest contribution to the team is their ability to shape the team's efforts into a united and practical course of action, and then push ahead energetically to turn ideas into action and practical reality.
- their greatest failings are:
  - their insensitivity to other people's feelings and needs
  - their ability to provoke, irritate and upset other people.

The Monitor Evaluator

Someone who fits the description of Monitor Evaluator is:

- **an analytical person**   They are particularly good at examining ideas (often in exhaustive detail) to analyse the strengths and weaknesses of each, and then forming an opinion based on their findings.
- **a cautious, unemotional person**   They don't have enthusiasms. They don't jump to conclusions. They don't act impulsively, or on instinct or gutfeeling.
- **a thorough person**   A Monitor Evaluator will leave no stone unturned if asked to analyse and evaluate data. Other team members may be screaming for

a decision, but the Monitor Evaluator will carefully, shrewdly and prudently weigh up all the pros and cons – no matter how long it takes.

■ their greatest contribution to the team is their ability to take an objective view when considering other people's ideas. Often, a Monitor Evaluator will save the team from a rash and costly error of judgement.

■ their greatest failings are:
   – their lack of enthusiasm, and their inability to inspire or motivate their team members
   – their lack of tact and diplomacy; if they consider someone's cherished idea and it seems likely to end in tears, the Monitor Evaluator will say so, bluntly and directly, without any frills attached.

The Team Worker

Someone who fits the description of Team Worker is:

■ **a sociable person**   They like people, and they like people to be happy together.

■ **a loyal person**   The team is really important to the Team Worker and they will work hard to preserve the team, and nurture team spirit, no matter how rocky the road becomes.

■ **a diplomatic person**   They are conscious of and concerned about the relationships within the team, and will make a real effort to pour oil on troubled waters when conflict occurs.

■ their greatest contribution to the team is their ability to support everyone, and keep the team functioning as smoothly and as harmoniously as is humanly possible.

■ their greatest failings are:
   – can be indecisive, particularly if they have to choose whether to put people and relationships first or tasks and objectives first.

The Implementer

Someone who fits the description of Implementer is:

■ **an organized person**   They enjoy turning ideas into action and producing the goods on time, within budget.

■ **a sensible, self-disciplined person**   Implementers are good at turning chaos into order, and take pleasure in working out schedules and devising budgets, systems and procedures.

■ their greatest contribution to the team is their organizing ability and their skill at turning airy-fairy ideas into concrete plans of action.

■ their greatest failings are:
   – their inflexibility and resistance to change.

The Completer

Someone who fits the description of Completer is:

- **an anxious person**   Although they may appear to be cool, calm and collected, inwardly they are worried to death in case something goes wrong. Their strategy for reassuring themselves that nothing will go wrong is to check, recheck and then double-check all the details.
- A Completer **never** assumes it will be 'all right on the night'.
- **a conscientious person**   If a Completer says they will do something, then you can rely on the fact that not only will it be done, but it will be done on time, and to a very high standard.
- their greatest contribution to the team is their ability to take care of the details and to make sure that a project doesn't sink into oblivion just because one signature is missing from a contract, or an important telephone call is forgotten.
- their greatest failings are:
  - their high expectations of themselves and everyone else on the team
  - their intolerance towards slapdash, careless, happy-go-lucky (and often highly creative) work.

In an ideal world, a perfect team would consist of at least eight people, each of whom would be comfortable operating in one of Belbin's eight team roles. This perfect mix is highly unlikely. In fact, you are much more likely to find teams composed of highly unsatisfactory combinations, such as:

- three Shapers and one Plant
- two Monitor Evaluators, two Completers and one Team Worker
- four Resource Investigators and one Monitor Evaluator
- three Plants and one Implementer.

Sometimes teams are brought together by circumstance or practicality, rather than best practice. If you are given a team of people, then you simply have to work with the individuals and seek to make the best of what you have got.

ACTIVITY 4

For the purpose of this activity imagine that, on your team, there are eight people, each one of whom is naturally one of Belbin's eight team types. Who is most likely to clash with whom, and why? Note your ideas on the chart below.

Team role	Most likely to come into conflict with which other team role(s)?	Most likely reasons for conflict
Plant		
Resource Investigator		
Co-ordinator		
Shaper		
Monitor Evaluator		
Team Worker		
Implementer		
Completer		

FEEDBACK

Some (although not all) potential areas of conflict between team roles are shown in the chart below.

Team role	Most likely to come into conflict with which other team role(s)?	Most likely reasons for conflict
Plant	Team Worker	Introverted Plants are often not particularly good team players and may not be keen to socialize.
	Shaper	Plants can find the Shaper's relentless energy and ambition just too much to take.
Resource Investigator	Monitor Evaluator	Resource Investigators are outgoing, optimistic people who can usually see all of the advantages and none of the snags. Dry, unemotional, analytical Monitor Evaluators tend to pour cold water on Resource Investigators' bright ideas. Resource Investigators are not strong on detail, and the
	Completer	Completer's obsession with getting things right can cause the Resource Investigator to quickly lose interest.
Co-ordinator	Team Worker	Co-ordinators are focused people and objectives are important to them. They can clash with Team Workers who put relationships top of the agenda, and objectives and results lower down.
Completer	Anyone and everyone who takes even a vaguely relaxed approach to the team, its tasks and its objectives.	Completers can be intolerant to anyone who does not meet their high standards.

Ways in which you can attempt to minimize conflict and maintain harmony on the team include:

- **Identify most likely areas of potential conflict.** Work out who you have on the team, and who is most likely to conflict with whom. Then separate the people who are most likely to clash. You can do this by sub-dividing the team into different sub-teams or working parties, each with responsibility for a different aspect of the project. In addition, try to ensure that at team meetings where everyone is present, you also have a Team Worker or Co-ordinator to keep the peace.
- **Reshuffle with another team or recruit.** This may involve talking to another team who has, say, two Plants, and who is prepared to swop a Plant for a Team Worker or a Completer. If this isn't feasible or possible, you may have to recruit a particular team role to join the team. Your *person specification* should clearly profile the team role for which you are looking.
- **Allocate the right kinds of work to the appropriate team roles.** Make sure that you allocate tasks according to skills, abilities and Team Role preferences. For example, don't ask the Plant to monitor the budget; don't expect the Resource Investigator to work alone in isolated splendour; don't ask the Shaper to undertake an especially tricky and sensitive negotiation with someone for whom he or she has scant respect.

You can complete detailed questionnaires which will identify your preferred team role (see *Information Toolbox* for references). However, what's more important is to use Belbin's theory to remind yourself that individual members of your team are very different and to try to tailor development activities to the needs and preferences of team members rather than assuming a 'one size fits all' approach.

LEARNING STYLES

When we learn we acquire new skills, knowledge or attitudes through the process of:

- experiencing (doing, hearing or reading about something)
- reflecting (thinking about what we have done, heard or read)
- forming abstract concepts and generalizations (drawing conclusions from our reflections)
- testing concepts in new situations (trying different things).

Figure 1.4 shows the loop that this process creates.

Figure 1.4 Kolb's learning cycle. Kolb, D.A. (1984) *Experimental Learning: Experience as the Source of Learning and Development*, Englewood Cliffs: Prentice Hall

In practice, the process works like this.

1   You decide to send an e-mail using your newly installed e-mail sending software programme. You do everything you are supposed to (you think), and click the 'send' button. (This is the experience.)

2   Later in the day you return to the e-mail software and discover, to your disappointment, that your carefully composed message has been returned to you with a curt on-screen note saying 'Unable to deliver – host address unknown.' You read the instruction book and check that you did everything right; you ask a colleague for their opinion and discuss what you did; you think hard about what might have gone wrong. (This is the reflecting part of the process.)

3   You decide, in the light of all the available information, that the problem occurred because you omitted the word 'Internet' at the start of the recipient's address. (You are forming abstract concepts and generalizations.)

4   You change the recipient's address to include the word 'Internet' and you click the 'send' button again. (You are testing concepts.)

At this point, anything can happen. If the recipient receives the e-mail then you will have **learned** to include the word Internet in the address. If – even with this change – the e-mail is returned to you, you will have to go through the whole process again, and again, and maybe even again to **learn** what it is you need to do.

Eventually you will become so familiar with the process of creating and sending e-mail that you no longer have to consult the manual, or even really think about what you are doing. You will have learned something new and there will be a relatively permanent change in behaviour that occurs as a result of practice or experience.

Regardless of whether you are:

- personally responsible for some aspect of the design and delivery of training
- responsible for managing the delivery of training opportunities presented by training specialists or external consultants
- required to undertake some staff development as part of your managerial role,

it is important for you to understand the learning cycle. Different people feel more comfortable in different areas of the learning cycle and you need to appreciate that different people learn in different ways, and at different speeds. For example:

- an **activist** learner feels most comfortable in the 'experiencing' part of the learning cycle.

  They learn best from:
  - handling problems, dealing with crises, tackling new challenges and experiences
  - getting involved in situations with other people where they can bounce ideas around and solve problems through teamwork
  - group learning activities such as business games, competitive teamwork task and role-playing exercises.

  They learn least from:
  - getting involved in assimilating, analysing and interpreting lots of 'messy' data
  - having to engage in solitary activities such as reading, writing or thinking on their own
  - formal learning tasks such as listening to lectures, reading or watching someone perform a task.

- A **reflective** learner feels most comfortable in the 'reflective' part of the learning cycle.

  They learn best from:
  - situations where they have ample time to prepare in advance so they can think things through before taking action or giving an opinion
  - preparing carefully considered and analysed reports
  - watching other people perform tasks and then thinking about what they have seen.

They learn least from:
- situations where they have to take shortcuts or produce superficial work
- being required to make decisions or reach conclusions based on insufficient data
- being forced into having to chair a meeting, lead a discussion or role-play in front of other people.

■ A **theoretical** learner feels most comfortable in the 'forming abstracts' part of the learning cycle. They like to know why they are doing something and how things work.

They learn best form:
- having the opportunity to question the basic methodology which has been used, or probe the assumptions made and the logic used to reach conclusions
- being able to listen to or read about ideas and concepts based on rationality and logic
- working with activities and tasks that are part of a system or model concept, or those firmly based on an accepted theory.

They learn least from:
- being thrown in at the deep end
- getting involved in situations (or structured learning activites) where there are high levels of ambiguity and uncertainty
- any activity, task or situation that they feel is shallow or gimmicky.

■ A **pragmatist** learner feels most comfortable in the 'testing concepts' part of the learning cycle.

They learn best from:
- situations in which they can focus on practical issues and activities such as drawing up action plans or giving advice or assistance
- situations where they can obtain coaching and feedback from a credible expert
- learning opportunities where there is an obvious link between the subject matter and their own work, and where they can apply what they have learned in a practical way within their organization.

They learn least from:
- learning opportunities that have no relevance to their job
- situations, ideas, concepts that seem purely theoretical without any practical, useful application
- formal learning opportunities where there is no apparent reward.

In practice, you may have noticed that you are personally drawn towards certain types of learning methods or that you simply find it easier to learn some things and difficult to learn others. For example, learning a new skill (say, using a multi-feature photocopier) may be difficult for you, and easy for John. Understanding, say, the difference between the accounting terms Internal Rate of Return and Net Present Value may be easy for you, and difficult for John. Generally John may prefer hands-on, experiential learning, whereas you may learn more easily from reflective study, working alone.

ACTIVITY 5

Having read the descriptions of the different learning styles, what do you feel is your preferred learning style?

FEEDBACK

It is possible to complete questionnaires which identify a person's preferred learning style – see the *Information Toolbox* for references. However, most people will immediately be able to identify with the situations they feel most comfortable in.

The secret of designing effective training and learning opportunities lies in building opportunities for learning which use all the styles of the learning cycle. Again, as with team roles, it is useful to be aware that people have different learning styles so that you are flexible in your approach to developing members of your team.

Learning summary

- Part of a manager's responsibility is developing team members. Manager's need to understand themselves and their team members so that they can tailor development activities.
- The four styles of leadership can be matched to the four categories of competence and commitment as follows:
  - Style 1: Directive (gives clear instructions) works best with low competence/high commitment.
  - Style 2: Coaching (talking things through) works best with some competence/low commitment.
  - Style 3: Supporting (show interest) works best with high competence/variable commitment.
  - Style 4: Delegating (trusts) works best with high competence/high commitment.
- The autocratic–democratic model of leadership looks at approaches to decision-making on a continuum from being directive (leader taking all decisions) to delegative (leader joins team in decision-making).
- The psychologist Dr Meredith Belbin has identified eight team roles which people adopt when they become part of a team.
- People cannot choose the team role they **naturally** adopt, although they can choose – when necessary – to adopt a secondary team role which fits their style, temperament and personality.
- The eight team roles are the:
  1 Plant
  2 Resource Investigator
  3 Co-ordinator
  4 Shaper
  5 Monitor Evaluator
  6 Team Worker
  7 Implementer
  8 Completer.
- When allocating work, always consider:
  - What is there to do?
  - Who is capable of doing it?
  - Who has the time?
  - Who needs the development?
- People have different preferred learning styles. Selecting a method of development which matches someone's preferred learning style will increase the likelihood of a successful learning outcome.

Into the workplace

You need to:

- recognize your preferred style of leadership
- identify characteristics of team members which are likely to affect how they can maximize the benefits of development opportunities.

References

1 Hersey P. & Blanchard K (1993) *Management of Organizational Behavior: Utilizing Human Resources*, Sixth edition, Prentice Hall
2 Tannenbaum R. & Scmidt W (1973) *How to Choose a Leadership Pattern*, Harvard Business Review

Section 2   Meeting development needs

Introduction

Before you can start the process of actually meeting staff development needs, it's important to find out precisely what those needs are. The old philosophy of 'Let's throw some money at the problem. If we give them some training that'll sort it out' is both outdated and totally unproductive.

Development should be carefully planned and meticulously organized to meet the real needs of both the individual and the organization. Anything less is a waste of time and money.

In this section of the workbook we will be focusing on:

- methods of identifying development needs
- features of effective development opportunities.

Informal or formal development?

Informal staff development often occurs because a senior member of staff spots talent and potential in a more junior member of staff. The senior person may, in an informal way, encourage that talent and potential by offering significant development opportunities as and when they occur.

CASE STUDY

Barbara, a senior manager in a publishing house, explains:

'I used to work as a Personal Assistant to a woman who seemed to think I was capable of doing much, much more ... her opinion, rather than mine, I have to say. She would give me tasks which I honestly believed I was incapable of doing – but I liked her enormously, and I didn't want to let her down. Also, I suppose part of me felt that if she thought I was capable of doing it, then maybe I could! Of course, as I successfully completed each new task my self-esteem grew. I began to see that I was more capable than I had believed – and that's when my confidence really kicked in and I became more ambitious. I owe everything to her, because of the opportunities she gave me to prove myself.'

Providing people with meaningful development opportunities can be nerve-wracking and, if your judgement is poor, even dangerous. For example, statements like:

- 'I'd like you to chair the meeting'
- 'I want you to make the presentation in New York'
- 'OK – it's your project, you set up the budget and manage it'
- 'You negotiate with the client',

if not properly thought through, can provide someone with a perfect opportunity to wreak total havoc in an organization as well as completely disregarding a person's preferred learning style. But, if you are sure of the person to whom you are delegating, and if you delegate properly – by setting clear parameters and monitoring carefully, but unobtrusively – these kinds of challenges can develop people rapidly. We look at delegating in more detail later in the workbook.

ACTIVITY 6

Take a few moments to reflect back over your own career to date before answering the following questions:

1 Who has been instrumental in providing development opportunities for you?

2 What were those development opportunities?

3 How has the successful completion of those development opportunities affected:
   (a) you, as an individual?

   (b) your career?

FEEDBACK

Opportunities are crucial to both individual development, and the development of the organization. Generally, capable people who have potential will rise to the challenge. Of course you may make some errors of judgement over the years. But, if you start in a small way by delegating important (but not critically important) tasks, you will be rewarded by the satisfaction of watching people develop their skills, abilities and career prospects.

Some managers make the mistake of withholding development opportunities from their staff. They do this because they worry that their subordinates, given half a chance, might ultimately challenge their own status and power.

CASE STUDY

Mike, a College Principal, explains how he was once caught in this trap:

'When I worked as a Head of Department I was responsible for a number of staff, many of whom were very competent people. I had worked my way up to the management team in the College and, I suppose, I guarded my position quite jealously. Looking back, I think I was worried that if other people were seen to be able to do what I could do, then it would reflect badly on me. Eventually, of course, I became worn out and totally stressed, because I was trying to do everything and shoulder all the responsibility. I felt defeated by it all and, very much in the spirit of 'Oh, what the hell', I started to offload work and delegate responsibility to the people I trusted most. Nothing dreadful happened! Instead, people began to blossom – use their initiative to make improvements and develop new and exciting projects. So, suddenly I had a department that was, for the most part, running smoothly and producing really good results. That success gave me the confidence to apply for, and get, my current job.'

Formal staff development involves structured training and learning opportunities for both individuals and teams.

ACTIVITY 7

List four kinds of structured training or learning opportunities that can be used to develop staff.

1

2

3

4

FEEDBACK

Formal, structured training and learning opportunities include:

- attending courses, seminars, lectures, workshops; reading books and watching videos
- working through an open learning or distance learning workbook or CD-ROM
- secondment to a different organization, location, function, department or section
- being coached by a more experienced colleague
- involvement in a formal mentoring programme within the organization.

Each of these opportunities has their own benefits and advantages and the choice should be dictated by the needs of:

- the individual
- the team
- the organization.

We look at different types of structured development activities in more detail in later sections.

Identifying development needs

Any identification of development needs has to be in the context of the wider organization. You need to know the standards, targets or objectives that the organization has set for itself. For example:

- increase market share by 10 per cent by December 2005
- decrease computer down-time by 20 per cent by January 2004
- improve internal communication systems by Spring 2005
- achieve Investors in People by May 2005.

You also need to know what your departmental objectives are and how they fit into the wider organization. Objectives at the levels within an organization should be aligned so that all parts of the organization are pulling in the same direction and contribute to the overall corporate objectives (Figure 2.1).

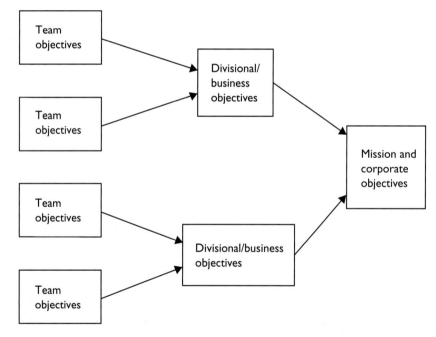

Figure 2.1

ACTIVITY 8

What are your departmental objectives? How do they complement the overall organization's objectives?

FEEDBACK

As a manager it's essential to know how you fit into the wider organization and have objectives for your team's performance. Objective setting is looked at in more detail in the workbook *The Performance Manager*.

Once you are clear about team's objectives, then you can begin to think about the skills, knowledge and attitudes the staff should possess in order to achieve the desired outcome.

IDENTIFYING DEVELOPMENT NEEDS IN THE PERFORMANCE MANAGEMENT PROCESS

As a manager you need to manage the performance of your team members. Organizations have a variety of processes and procedures which often form part, or all, of an appraisal and work review process. The aim of performance management is as follows:

■ To review previously set work objectives with a team member
■ To set new work objectives
■ To identify development needs and decide how they can be met

The identification of work objectives will contribute towards the overall team's objectives. For each work objective it is important to consider whether the team member has all the necessary skills and knowledge to achieve it. For example:

CASE STUDY

During a performance review with her line manager it was agreed that one of Helen's work objective would be:

– To disseminate information about the Disability Discrimination Act (DDA) to customers using services from January.

This immediately identified a development need for Helen as she would have to understand the DDA and its implications for their customers. Therefore two development objectives were identified:

– understand the DDA and its implications (by end of September)
– present information about the DDA to the rest of the team (by end of October).

Once development objectives have been set the method of meeting the development objective needs to be agreed. For example, it may be agreed that Helen needs to attend an external training course and then be coached by her line manager to plan and deliver a presentation about the DDA to the rest of the team.

ACTIVITY 9

Consider the way you review the performance of your team. Do you regularly meet with each team member to:

❏ review previously set work objectives?
❏ agree individual work objectives with each team member?
❏ identify any development needs resulting from each work objectives?
❏ set development objectives?
❏ select appropriate development opportunities with team members?

FEEDBACK

It's important that a record is kept of any performance management meeting. Each team member should have a working document in which they record work objectives and a personal development plan which is reviewed regularly.

IDENTIFYING DEVELOPMENT NEEDS BY TRAINING NEEDS ANALYSIS

A full analysis of training needs, sometimes referred to as Training Needs Analysis (TNA) is usually used when an organization seeks to:

■ provide staff with completely new skills or knowledge
■ improve or update existing staff skills, knowledge or attitude in order to enhance current performance.

The three key questions:

1 What does he or she know?
2 What does he or she need to know?
3 What training or learning would best close the gap?

are asked in respect of each individual member of staff within the organization, no matter how senior or how junior that person might be. Because of the size and scope of this kind of project a full analysis of training needs is normally only undertaken when:

- a brand new organization is to be created
- there is product or service diversification which requires staff to acquire a range of new knowledge and skills
- the company is seeking Investors in People accreditation
- the organization is teetering on the brink of disaster and it is felt that a major new training initiative is the only solution.

Methods used for identifying training needs include:

Issuing questionnaires

Providing the questionnaires are carefully designed by someone who has the right kind of expertise, they can provide a great deal of useful information. Figure 2.2 is a brief example of a training needs analysis questionnaire.

Name:	
Job title:	
Date:	
So far, what training have you received in Windows XP software?	
Is there any additional aspect of Windows XP software training you feel you would benefit from?	
How often do you use Windows XP?	
For what purpose do you most often use Windows XP?	
What problems do you most often encounter when using Windows XP?	
When problems occur, what actions do you usually take?	
For you, what is the most difficult part of using Windows XP?	
How useful do you find the Windows XP instruction manual?	
How often do you consult the instruction manual?	
What changes of additions to the manual would be most useful to you?	

Figure 2.2

Journal keeping

This process involves asking each member of staff to keep a work journal in which they record each task completed and each problem encountered. The journals are subsequently analysed to identify training needs. The main drawback with this technique is that even though people may set out with the best of intentions, journal keeping is time-consuming and requires focus and attention to detail. Important information can easily be omitted, so the journal may, in the end, prove to be a worthless document.

Observation

Using this approach, team members are observed as they carry out specific tasks. The observer identifies the skills and knowledge used, assesses the level of performance and analyses the skills and knowledge needed. Again, this is a time-consuming and laborious technique, particularly if a large number of staff are involved.

Assessment

Observation is an example of an assessment process, but there are other options available. Tests, simulations and case studies are often used, sometimes in the context of structured assessment centres.

ACTIVITY 10

Provide the information requested in the chart below, using a separate sheet of paper if you prefer, in order to ensure confidentiality.

Note: This activity should relate to members of your team – those people for whose development you have some measure of responsibility. Complete a separate chart for each team member.

NAME:	JOB TITLE:	
■ Date on which I identified training needs: ■ Methods I used to obtain the information: 		
Existing skills and knowledge	Proposed training intended to close the skills and knowledge gap	Required skills and knowledge
■	■	■
■	■	■
■	■	■
■	■	■
■	■	■

FEEDBACK

It's good practice to keep a record of all discussions related to the individual development of your team members. Development is an on-going activity where new opportunities are selected to build on existing skills and knowledge.

Investors in People

Investors in People (often referred to as IiP) is a government initiative devised to help organizations develop their people, through training and learning opportunities, in order to achieve the organization's business objectives.

Any organization wishing to achieve Investors in People must meet four principal requirements:

1 **Public commitment from the top to develop all employees to achieve the organization's business objectives.** This means that there must be a public commitment, from the most senior people in the business, to develop all staff. This must go far beyond a token statement of intent. Genuine commitment to IiP must:

   - cascade down from every senior manager
   - be written into the company's strategic plan
   - be supported by public notices of commitment
   - be reinforced by regular meetings to encourage and support the process.

2 **Regular reviews of the training and development needs of all employees.** IiP requires companies to regularly review training and development needs against business objectives, as well as regularly undertaking a review of individual staff member's training and development needs. This review may be done either through training needs analysis or performance appraisal.

   In addition, managers must verify that they are competent to develop other people. This may be done through their own performance appraisal, through assessment against the Management Standards Centre (MSC) management standards or through gaining a National Vocational Qualification (NVQ).

3 **Continuing action to train and develop individuals on recruitment and throughout their employment.** Companies hoping to gain IiP must:

   - have an effective induction programme for new employees
   - provide new employees with the training and development they need to do their job
   - ensure that existing employees are developed in line with business objectives.

Investors in People requires that all employees are made aware of the development opportunities which are open to them. These may include:

   - special projects, work shadowing, job rotation, secondment
   - courses, open learning, coaching, mentoring.

In an organization seeking IiP accreditation, managers have a responsibility to encourage and support employees in identifying and meeting their job-related development needs.

4   Regular evaluation of the investment in training and development to assess achievement and improve its future effectiveness. A company seeking IiP accreditation must evaluate:

■   how its development of people is contributing to business goals and targets
■   whether or not the development action taken is effective.

In addition to completing post-training evaluation questionnaires, organizations can evaluate training through:

■   discussion at performance appraisal
■   team de-briefing sessions
■   meetings between individual members of staff and their line manager.

As part of the IiP process, organizations need to compile a portfolio which contains evidence that action is being taken to meet the 4 principal requirements.

Typical steps to achieving IiP status would include:

1 Read and absorb the IiP Standard so that you clearly understand (a) what is required, and (b) the implications for your organization and its staff.

2 Link the Standard and your organization's Strategic Plan so that training and development are firmly on the agenda.

3 Appoint an IiP Co-ordinator to co-ordinate and administer the programme. Ideally, this would be someone who has expertise in the area of training and development.

4 Run a full analysis of training needs to find out (a) where people are now, and (b) where people need to be if they are to be able to meet the company's business objectives.

5 Produce an Action Plan to meet the four principal IiP requirements and have this agreed by senior management.

6 Set up a Steering Group composed of people at different levels and from different functions within the company. The role of the Steering Group should be to provide help and support with the implementation of the programme, monitor progress and channel feedback.

7 Make the commitment, in writing, to the appropriate Learning Skills Council, once you know your organization's staff are with you.

8 Communicate throughout the business and let everyone know what IiP is all about; what it means for individuals, teams and the company as a whole; let people know what is contained in the IiP Action Plan.

9 Plan the training and development opportunities by deciding what is going to happen, to whom, when, and the way in which the success of each opportunity is to be evaluated.

10 Assign and allocate resources – finance for the training budget, space, equipment and, of course, management time.

11 Gather evidence to prove that the company is meeting the IiP requirements. An assessor will visit your organization to meet staff and also to examine the portfolio of evidence.

12 Monitor progress on a regular basis, (at least two or three times a year), to make sure that everything is happening when it is supposed to happen, and in the way in which it's supposed to happen.

13 Set up a sample assessment. Ask your IiP adviser to run a sample assessment to check how close you are to achieving the required Standard. This will enable you to make any necessary adjustments prior to the formal assessment.

14 Prepare for assessment. Assessment is carried out through: (a) examination of the portfolio of evidence; (b) interviews with your staff, carried out by accredited assessors. The assessors will discuss IiP and ask questions about the four IiP principles.

15 Keep going. Once your organization has been awarded IiP status it is vital to keep going, because there will be periodic assessments to ensure that your company still meets the IiP requirements.

The next activity will give you an opportunity to think about the way in which staff development needs are currently identified within your organization.

ACTIVITY 11

Consider the following questions and note down your answers.

1   Currently, what system, method, process or technique is used within your organization to identify:

(a) individual training and development needs?

(b) team training and development needs?

2   How are individual and team training and development needs matched to corporate objectives?

3   How do you identify your own training and development needs?

4   What contribution do you personally make to the process of identifying staff training and development needs?

5   What changes or improvements would you make to the systems and procedures currently used in your organization to identify and meet training and development needs?

FEEDBACK

Even if your organization isn't involved in IiP, the features of IiP accreditation described above gives a model of good practice to any organization wishing to improve its people development practices.

The remaining sections of the workbook focus on specific development methods. We look at:

- planning and running training sessions
- coaching
- delegating
- mentoring.

Learning summary

- Developing people is the process of enabling individuals to improve existing and acquire new:
  - skills
  - knowledge
  - attitudes.
- Staff development can be:
  - informal and organic – offering people development opportunities as and when those opportunities arise
  - formal and structured – a planned programme offering structured training and learning opportunities to individuals and teams.
- The identification of development needs should be part of a performance management process.
- Training needs analysis is a process which addresses three key questions:
  - what does he or she know?
  - what does he or she need to know?
  - what training or learning would best close the gap?
- An analysis of staff training needs can be undertaken through:
  - interviews
  - questionnaires
  - journals
  - observation.
- The four principal requirements of the Investors in People programme are:
  - public commitment from the top to develop all employees to achieve the organization's business objectives
  - regular reviews of the training and development needs of all employees
  - continuing action to train and develop individuals on recruitment and throughout their employment
  - regular evaluation of the investment in training and development to assess achievement and improve its future effectiveness.

Into the workplace

You need to:

- review how you identify development needs within your team.

Section 3   Planning and running training sessions

Introduction

Within the best organizations – those which have made a serious commitment to staff development – training is not solely the responsibility of the training department. The training department is seen as a resource with managers taking responsibility for the development of their teams. Everyone in the organization, from the top-down, takes responsibility for making sure that staff development needs are met through the most effective and most relevant training and learning opportunities.

In this section of the workbook we are focusing on the design and delivery of effective training so that you will be in a better position to either prepare and run a training session, or assess and evaluate the effectiveness of training within your organization.

For the sake of clarity and simplicity, in this section, the word 'trainer' is used to describe someone who presents information about any topic or skill, to a group of people, in a way so that learning will take place.

Features of effective training

The secret of designing effective training and learning opportunities lies in building each of the following factors in to the training event, in equal proportion:

- learning objectives
- variety and involvement
- relevant content
- feedback and guidance
- different kinds of learning opportunity
- time to absorb information and practise new skills.

LEARNING OBJECTIVES

Learning objectives are statements that clearly explain what learners will know or be able to do when they have completed the training. The three main purposes of learning objectives are that they:

- give the training designer a structure and framework upon which to build a training event
- let the learners know what to expect from the training
- enable everyone involved – trainers, learners, interested managers – to evaluate whether or not the training has been successful and achieved the learning objectives.

Learning objectives should be easy to understand and should state, clearly and concisely, what learners should be able to do when they have completed the training. For example:

- design a critical path analysis chart
- demonstrate three different techniques for closing a sale
- explain the difference between variable and fixed costs
- describe the benefits of National Vocational Qualifications
- prepare a report describing the benefits of experiential learning
- analyse our regional sales statistics for 2004/2005.

When creating learning objectives, avoid words such as 'know' and 'understand', for example:

- know how to listen effectively
- understand the difference between profit and loss.

'Know' and 'understand' as learning objectives are difficult to measure. What does someone have to do to show they know or understand something? If outcomes are hard to measure then it follows that success or failure will be difficult to evaluate.

ACTIVITY 12

For the purpose of this activity imagine that it has been decided that everyone in the management team in your organization would benefit from a course in Communication Skills. The aim of the course is to ensure that, after the training, managers will be able to use clear verbal communication.

Your task is to prepare a list of five learning objectives which will:

a   help the trainer to design the course
b   tell the participants what they will be able to do and know after the training
c   provide a benchmark for success against which the learning can be measured.

At the end of the course participants will be able to:

1

2

3

4

5

FEEDBACK

Your list of learning objectives may include some of the following:

- give clear instructions
- explain complex information in a clear and straightforward manner
- answer questions thoroughly
- demonstrate effective listening skills
- use active listening skills
- use a range of questioning techniques
- ask appropriate questions to discover relevant information
- summarize the content of a conversation
- explain the difference between 'open' and 'closed' questions
- describe five characteristics of effective verbal communication.

Once the learning objectives have been decided, then the person who is designing the training event can decide what information and practical exercises should be included so that learners will be able to achieve the desired outcomes.

VARIETY AND INVOLVEMENT

Anyone who has sat on a hard chair in a stuffy, overheated room listening to 6 hours of 'chalk and talk' knows only too well that learning something new can be an excruciatingly boring experience.

Equally, given an interested and interesting presenter together with a range of varied learning exercises, learning can be an enjoyable and stimulating activity.

The average attention span of most people (no matter how motivated or intelligent they might be) is between 10 and 20 minutes, maximum. After that, people 'switch off'. Not necessarily because they want to switch off, but because that is the maximum amount of time people can give to absorbing new information. In practice, this means that a trainer who gives a chalk and talk lecture for longer than twenty minutes is wasting everyone's time.

ACTIVITY 13

Reflect back on the most interesting, challenging, enjoyable and informative training in which you have been involved as a learner. Note down, in the space below, four different training techniques or activities which were used by the trainer to provide variety and involvement for the participants on the course.

1

2

3

4

FEEDBACK

You may have experienced some, or all, of the following techniques:

- working as a member of a team, in competition with another team
- working as a member of a small syndicate of perhaps three or four people
- working in a trio where two people practise a skill, and the third person observes and comments
- working as one half of a partnership
- working as an individual, in competition with everyone else in the learning group.

You may have participated in one or more of the following activities:

- creative thinking – where everyone's contribution, no matter how outrageous or apparently irrelevant, is cheerfully accepted and, possibly, used to spark additional, creative ideas from others in the group
- creation of lists of ideas in response to specific questions asked by the group's trainer or facilitator
- group discussion
- research and presentation of information
- practice/demonstration of a skill
- problem solving – perhaps using case studies.

No matter what the topic or who the learners are (whether junior shopfloor staff or members of the Board), providing training that is varied, and which requires learner involvement, is the key to success.

RELEVANT CONTENT

Training should be relevant and pitched at an appropriate level for the learners. For instance, participants who have been booked onto a health and safety course do not want to know about the history of trade unionism; learners looking forward to updating their time management skills do not want a detailed explanation of Critical Path Analysis, and the senior management team, keen to improve internal communications, do not want to know which system is currently used to allocate spaces in the staff car park.

Learners need to feel that the content of the training (the information being presented) and the practical exercises and activities in which they are participating:

- are current and up to date
- are useful and practical
- will help them to be more efficient and effective
- can be used by them in their work
- may contribute, in a positive way, to their career prospects.

FEEDBACK AND GUIDANCE

Everyone, from the CEO down, needs to know how they are doing. Getting the answers to questions like:

- Am I doing OK?
- Am I doing as well as – or better than – my colleagues?
- Am I meeting other people's expectations?

is particularly important when people are involved in acquiring new knowledge or learning new skills.

Learners who do not receive constructive feedback and helpful guidance in a training situation may quickly become disenchanted, and can think:

- This trainer doesn't care how I'm doing – so the course can't be that important.
- I'm not getting any feedback – I must be doing really badly – so there's no point in trying … I'll just give up now.
- This trainer doesn't like me – so why should I like them?
- Does this trainer know what they're doing?

Acknowledging learners' efforts and providing encouragement and support are key parts of the trainer's or facilitator's role.

DIFFERENT KINDS OF LEARNING OPPORTUNITY

As you saw Section 1, different people prefer to learn in different ways. A well-designed course, seminar or workshop will take account of these differences, and will provide a range of different learning opportunities to suit everyone. For example:

- hands-on exercises to help the Activists to learn
- demonstrations and practical examples to help the Reflectors to learn
- clear, logical explanations to help the Theorists to learn
- discussion and real-life examples of how the training topic can be applied in a practical way at work, to help the Pragmatists to learn.

TIME TO ABSORB INFORMATION AND PRACTISE NEW SKILLS

Correct pacing is vital to the success of a training course, workshop or seminar. 'Pacing' is really about the speed at which new topics are introduced, and the amount of time given to each. Courses that are too slow spend far too long on one discussion or one activity, so that participants get bored and restless and begin to wish they were back at work, doing something useful. Courses that are too fast rush, helter-skelter, from one topic to another, nothing is covered in depth, no one has time to consider the information, and everyone leaves the training none the wiser for the experience.

Effective trainers and facilitators provide opportunities for people to reflect on what has been learned and to think about how they can apply the principles, in practice, to real-life situations. They do this through:

- discussions
- question and answer sessions
- providing relevant case studies and examples which demonstrate how the principle works in practice
- allowing frequent breaks which give learners the opportunity to process and absorb new information.

Planning a training event

From time to time you may, as a manager, be required to plan a training session. Or, you may have to assess and evaluate the way a training session has been designed and delivered by an external consultant, or someone from your own organization's training function.

Effective training on any topic will address the key questions:

- What do they know, and what can they do?
- What do they need to know, and need to do?

IDENTIFY THE GAPS AND WRITE THE LEARNING OBJECTIVES

When planning a training session your first step is to identify the gap, and then write the learning objectives, for example:

By the end of the session learners will be able to:

- write clear and concise business reports
- present numerical data in an easy to understand, graphical format
- prepare a range of standard format business letters.

KNOWLEDGE CONTENT

Once you have written the learning objectives, your next step is to think about the knowledge the learners will need in order to achieve the desired outcomes, for example:

Write clear and concise business reports – knowledge:

- use double spacing on A4 paper
- keep sentences short
- divide information into sections and label each clearly with a different heading.

This is the **theory** part of the course, and this information is usually delivered by the trainer using a variety of techniques including:

- overhead projector acetates
- flipcharts
- paper-based information, which is handed out
- question and answer session.

PRACTICAL CONTENT

Your next step is to consider what kind of **practical** learning activities you can provide for the learners so that they can become actively involved, for example:

Write clear and concise business reports – activities:

- in pairs, read through this report, comment on its clarity and suggest ways in which it might be improved
- in teams, prepare a one-page report on 'Where our company will be 5 years from now'
- as a group, identify the key elements of a clear and concise business report.

PLANNING THE TIME

Once you know the:

- theory you will be presenting to the group
- type and number of activities you will be asking the group to participate in.

Your next task is to work out a rough timetable for the session. An example training session timetable is shown in Figure 3.1.

Morning 9.30 a.m. to 1 p.m.	Afternoon 2 p.m. to 5.30 p.m.
■ **9.30–10.00** Group introductions	■ **2.00–2.15** Trainer input – recap on main learning points from morning
■ **10.00–10.30** Creative thinking exercise – key points of a good report	■ **2.15–3.30** Team activity: two teams, each preparing a one-page report on 'Where our business will be five years from now?'
■ **10.30–1045** Discussion	■ **3.30–3.45** Feedback and discussion
■ **10.45–11.15** Break	■ **3.45–4.00** Coffee
■ **11.15–11.45** Trainer input and presentation of theory – Powerpoint	■ **4.00–4.45** Individual activity: write a one-page report on 'The key learning points from this course'
■ **11.45–12.30** Pairs activity – comments and suggestions on a business report (samples provided)	■ **4.45–5.30** Presentation and discussion of the reports
■ **12.30–1.00** Feedback and discussion **1.00** Lunch	■ **5.30** Participants complete course evaluation reports; trainer closes the course

Figure 3.1   Timetable for one-day session on writing business reports

PLANNING THE RESOURCES

As anyone who has ever delivered a training session knows only too well, having the right amount of the right kind of resources will make the difference between a smooth-running, enjoyable event and one that is chaotic and irritating for everyone concerned.

ACTIVITY 14

Consider the timetable shown in Figure 3.1, and complete the chart below by noting the resources you would need if you were planning to deliver this training session to a group of 14 people.

Activity	Resources needed
9.30–10.00 Group introductions	■
10.00–10.30 Creative thinking exercise – key points of a good report	■
10.30–10.45 Discussion	■
11.15–11.45 Trainer input and presentation of theory – Powerpoint	■
11.45–12.30 Pairs activity – comments and suggestions on a business report – samples provided	■
12.30–1.00 Feedback and discussion	■
2.00–2.15 Trainer input – re-cap on main learning points from this morning	■
2.15–3.30 Team activity: two teams in competition – preparing a one-page report on 'Where our business will be 5 years from now'	■
3.30–3.45 Feedback and discussion	■
4.00–4.45 Individual activity: write a one-page report on 'The key learning points from this course'	■
4.45–5.30 Presentation and discussion of the reports	■
5.30 Participants complete course evaluation reports; trainer closes the course	■

FEEDBACK

Your completed chart should look something like this.

Activity	Resources needed
9.30–10.00 Group introductions	■ Name cards for trainer and participants ■ PowerPoint equipment(backup OHP) ■ Slide showing learning objectives for the course
10.00–10.30 Creative thinking exercise – key points of a good report	■ flipcharts and easels ■ marker pens ■ scrap paper ■ biros, pencils ■ Blu-Tak
11.15–11.45 Trainer input and presentation of theory – Powerpoint	■ PowerPoint equipment ■ Key Points and notes to be handed out × 14 sets
11.45–12.30 Pairs activity – comments and suggestions on a business report – samples provided	■ sample reports to be handed out to pairs × 7 ■ flipcharts ■ marker pens ■ Blu-Tak
2.15–3.30 Team activity: two teams in competition – preparing a one-page report on 'Where our business will be 5 years from now'	■ scrap paper ■ biros and pencils ■ dictionary × 2 ■ thesaurus × 2
4.00–4.45 Individual activity: write a one-page report on 'The key learning points from this course'	■ scrap paper ■ biros and pencils ■ dictionary ■ thesaurus ■ 3 × 5 record cards × 100
4.45–5.30 Presentation and discussion of the reports	■ flipcharts ■ marker pens ■ Blu-Tak
5.30 Participants complete course evaluation reports; trainer closes the course	Key Points and notes to be handed out × 14 sets course evaluation reports × 14

PREPARING THE RESOURCES

The next step is to prepare the resources you will need for the session. This may involve:

- creating slides, which can be done by hand or by using a specialist presentation computer software programs such as, PowerPoint, Freelance or PageMaker or OHP acetates. Used in conjunction with a trainer's words, slides showing key learning points, pictures or graphs reinforce what is being said and help learners to remember the information. Slides:
  - explain, amplify or clarify points
  - hold attention, help concentration and aid retention
  - add interest and variety.
- writing handouts, which are usually best produced on a word-processor and then photocopied. Handouts should be:
  - straightforward, easy to understand, jargon-free
  - clear and easy to read
  - contain relevant information and key learning points.
- gathering together the flipcharts and pads, pens, evaluation sheets and any other equipment, stationery, tools or props you intend to use.

PREPARING THE TRAINING ROOM

The training room should be:

- well lit (preferably by daylight) and well ventilated
- heated or cooled to an appropriate temperature
- sufficiently large to contain, comfortably, all the participants, the trainer and the equipment
- provide the right number of comfortable chairs and tables
- clean and tidy.

These are important factors and every care and attention should be paid to the comfort and well-being of the participants. Unhappy, uncomfortable people who are too hot, too cold or overcrowded will not and cannot concentrate and focus on anything other than how hot, or cold, or crowded or uncomfortable they are. For the sake of the participants, and in the cause of self-preservation, trainers should not ignore these basic needs.

Delivering the training

You have designed the course, prepared the resources, booked the room and informed the delegates that you will be expecting them to arrive on a particular day at a specific time. All that's left to do is facilitate the event itself.

ACTIVITY 15

Cast your mind back over the training events which you have attended, in the past, as a participant. Think about the qualities and skills needed by an effective trainer, and also some of the qualities and skills you may have seen demonstrated by an ineffective trainer. Then complete the chart below.

Skills and qualities of an effective trainer	Skills and qualities of an ineffective trainer
1	1
2	2
3	3
4	4
5	5
6	6

FEEDBACK

Effective trainers:

- are comfortable with and knowledgeable about the topic they are presenting
- make sure they are well prepared and well rehearsed
- welcome the participants and put people at their ease
- agree the ground rules with the group – breaks, smoking, timing, etc.
- start the session with an appropriate exercise to 'break the ice' and settle the participants into a learning frame of mind
- use equipment – overhead projector, flipchart, video, etc. – confidently and competently
- speak clearly, write legibly
- invite questions and answer them carefully and intelligently
- involve everyone – even those who have 'done this before'; 'haven't got time for this'; 'can't see the point'; or 'know it won't work in practice'
- respect the participants – they recognize they are dealing with adults, and they behave accordingly
- pay equal attention to all contributions
- watch for signs of boredom or stress – and take appropriate action by adjusting the pace, or varying the activities
- remain even tempered and good humoured (under all circumstances)
- offer useful and constructive feedback, guidance and advice
- adapt the session (if necessary) to meet the needs of the group.

Ineffective trainers often:

- ignore the mood or needs of the group and simply soldier on, regardless
- pay attention only to the brightest or the most amenable participants
- use inappropriate humour to make jokes at the expense of participants
- are sarcastic, bullying, critical, judgemental, condescending and/or patronizing
- waste time and/or go over time
- talk incessantly
- refuse to answer questions
- assume that if the participants don't understand, it's the participants' fault, and nothing to do with the trainer
- allow the strongest personalities in the group to take over
- allow their own boredom, tiredness or irritation to shine out like a beacon to everyone in the room
- pretend they 'know it all', when they don't.

Evaluating training

Evaluation is the process of analysing the value of something. Sound evaluation of any training intervention (e.g. course, workshop, seminar, open/distance learning programme, etc.) is equally important for:

- individual participants
- the training function
- the organization.

ACTIVITY 16

What are the benefits of evaluating the success or failure of training?

List two benefits of evaluation for the individual participant:

1

2

List two benefits of evaluation for the training function:

1

2

List two benefits of evaluation for the business as a whole:

1

2

FEEDBACK

Benefits of evaluation for individual participants

Learners can:

- safely, and without fear of reprisal, give their honest opinion on all aspects of the training intervention, e.g. the facilities, the trainer, the content of the course, the level of participation, whether or not they achieved the outcomes stated in the learning objectives
- give feedback as to whether or not there is likely to be a change or improvement in their knowledge, level of skill or attitude, as a result of the training
- indicate whether or not different or additional, similar, training might be of value in the future.

Benefits of evaluation for the training function

Trainers (and training managers) can:

- assess individual competence, e.g. a trainer's ability to:
  - design and prepare a training session
  - deliver a training session
  - enable learners to acquire a relatively permanent change in behaviour that occurs as a result of practice or experience
- identify success, and repeat successful training interventions
- identify failure and make appropriate changes to future sessions
- identify likely training needs for the future.

Benefits of evaluation for the organization

Organizations can:

- see where the organization is in terms of staff development as it relates to the business' objectives and long-term strategic plan
- use evaluation as a basis for planning future staff development needs
- gain relevant feedback on the effectiveness of the training function
- if appropriate, progress towards the achievement of the Investors in People Standard (as evaluation is a key IiP requirement).

HOW TO EVALUATE?

Happy sheets

At the conclusion of most training events, participants are asked to complete a Course Evaluation Form, often referred to as a 'Happy Sheet'.

Some Course Evaluation Sheets have space for the participant's name and job title, although others do not ask for this information – on the basis that guaranteed anonymity is more likely to produce honest feedback from learners.

De-briefing sessions

Following on from a training event, many organizations hold a de-briefing session at which the participants are invited to discuss all aspects of the training. A key feature of many of these meetings is not only to ask 'How did it go?' but also to find out 'What would you like next?'

Training evaluation, to be meaningful, should really be carried out:

- immediately after the event – as timely feedback can signpost changes which need to be made for future sessions, and
- 3 to 6 months after the event – to check whether or not the training has actually been transferred to the workplace by the participants and has affected their knowledge, skills and ability. Training that doesn't stick, and which doesn't result in a relatively permanent change in behaviour is, at best, not good value for money and, at worst, a complete waste of time and energy.

ACTIVITY 17

1   What systems, processes and procedures are currently used, in your organization, to evaluate training?

2   How successful are these systems, processes and procedures in practice?

Highly successful   ❏
Reasonably successful   ❏
Not at all successful   ❏

Please give your reasons for your selected response.

3   What changes or improvements would you make to improve the effectiveness of current training evaluation systems, processes and procedures?

Learning summary

- The key factors that enable learners to learn are:
  - learning objectives
  - relevant content
  - opportunities to learn which suit their own style and speed
  - feedback and guidance
  - time to practise new skills and absorb new information
  - varied teaching and learning techniques
  - involvement in the learning process (active rather than passive).
- Planning a training event involves:
  - identifying the gaps between know/don't know and can do/can't do
  - writing appropriate learning objectives
  - identifying the knowledge content of the session (theory)
  - identifying the practical content of the session (exercises and activities)
  - planning the time
  - planning the resources
  - preparing the resources
  - preparing the training room
  - delivering the training
  - evaluating the training.
- Effective trainers:
  - have in-depth knowledge of the topic they are presenting – they know their stuff
  - use equipment and resources competently
  - speak clearly and write legibly
  - put learners at their ease
  - invite questions and answer them thoroughly
  - offer constructive feedback, guidance and advice
  - involve everyone and pay equal attention to everyone
  - respect the participants
  - remain calm, cheerful and even tempered throughout
  - adapt the session to meet the needs of the participants.
- Ineffective and unprofessional trainers:
  - ignore the needs of the group
  - pay attention to some participants and ignore others
  - use inappropriate humour
  - are sarcastic, bullying, critical, judgemental, condescending, patronizing
  - waste time and/or go over time
  - talk incessantly
  - are unable to answer questions
  - take the view that what they are doing is adequate, and if people don't understand it is not the facilitator's fault
  - allow the strongest, most talkative participants to take over

- – show their boredom, tiredness or irritation
- – pretend that they know it all.
- ■ Organizations can evaluate the effectiveness of training events by:
  - – asking participants to complete Course Evaluation Sheets (often referred to as Happy Sheets)
  - – de-briefing sessions:
    - (a) immediately after the event
    - (b) 3 to 6 months after the event.

Into the workplace

You need to:

- ■ Plan, deliver and evaluate a training event.

Section 4 Coaching

Introduction

Coaching is a key method that line managers can use to develop their staff. It's ideal when you have a team member who has some ability to perform a task but little experience and it can be fully integrated into the normal work routine. In this section of the workbook we'll looking at the ways in which you can develop and improve your coaching skills in order to get the best from your staff.

What does coaching mean to you?

Perhaps, as a manager, you already undertake a fair amount of coaching as part and parcel of your everyday working life. Or, maybe, you feel that coaching others is an intrusion on your time and best left to the 'experts'.

Use the following activity as an opportunity to reflect on your views about coaching.

ACTIVITY 18

Consider the statements below and choose the statement most accurately reflecting your views.

1 If someone can't do the job to the required standard,
   then it's their responsibility to make sure they improve.   ❑

   Every manager has a responsibility for staff development.   ❑

2 Busy managers simply don't have time to coach staff.   ❑

   Coaching is so important that it has to be a priority for managers.   ❑

3 Coaching can be used to help someone to develop any
   kind of knowledge, skill or attitude.   ❑

   Coaching is really only useful for teaching straightforward skills.   ❑

4 The best way to develop staff is to make sure that they
   have formal training opportunities, delivered by training experts.   ❑

   Increased responsibility, more complex tasks, reviews, special
   projects, discussions, briefings, feedback sessions are the
   most effective techniques for developing staff.   ❑

5 An effective coach spends most time watching and listening.   ❑

   An effective coach spends most time telling and showing.   ❑

6 Learning is an organic process – it just happens.   ❑

   Coaching is a necessary part of the learning process.   ❑

FEEDBACK

1 **Every manager has a responsibility for staff development.**   Taking responsibility for developing the people on the team comes with the territory. Successful managers pay attention to enhancing their staff's skills and abilities, because they know that, ultimately, they will reap the rewards of developing their people, e.g. improved productivity, higher levels of motivation, increased creativity and innovation, and so on.

2 **Coaching is so important that it has to be a priority for managers.**   It is certainly true that some people, when left to their own devices, will create their own development opportunities. Most people, though, need encouragement, support, advice, guidance and constructive criticism to help them see how they could improve their job performance. Staff development, by and large, doesn't just happen. Managers have to take the lead and help it to happen.

3 **Coaching can be used to help someone develop any kind of knowledge, skill or attitude.**   People can:

- acquire knowledge through discussion, and through guidance to read the appropriate books, journals or reports
- acquire skills by watching a skilled person perform a task

■   acquire attitudes by having those attitudes 'modelled' for them – 'this is how I do it, now you copy me'.

4   **Increased responsibility, more complex tasks, reviews, special projects, discussions, briefings, feedback sessions are the most effective techniques for developing staff.**   Whilst formal training interventions are a key aspect of staff development, most people learn best on the job, in real life situations, where what they say and do really matters.

5   **An effective coach spends most time watching and listening.**   Whilst people need support, encouragement and practical advice, coaching is not about constantly jumping in and taking over the job – unless, of course, you see a disaster just waiting to happen. Remember that one of the key aspects of a learning organization is allowing people to make genuine mistakes, providing they are prepared to learn from them.

6   **Coaching is a necessary part of the learning process.**   Everyone needs a role model, and everyone needs to know:

■   how to do something

■   whether or not they are doing it 'right'

■   what they could do to 'do it better'.

People don't learn in isolation. They learn through experience, through modelling the way other people deal with the experience, through trying things in a different way, and through receiving appropriate and useful feedback on their performance.

Setting coaching targets

As the result of observing someone going about their job, or as the outcome of a work review you, as a manager, may have to set specific coaching targets for certain members of staff. For example, you might think to yourself:

■   'I'll have to do something about Joanna's filing'

■   'If Tom's presentations don't improve we'll all be in hospital with terminal boredom'

■   'Mike's going to have to manage his time better'

■   'Louise will have to learn to speak up when she's on the 'phone'.

In order to achieve a specific improvement, you need to set a specific target, which is Simple, Measurable, Achievable and Realistic. For example:

■   'I'll have to do something about Joanna's filing – I want her to store items numerically and cross reference them with alphabetical index cards'

■   'If Tom's presentations don't improve we'll all be in hospital with terminal boredom – I want him to present information concisely, and in a logical order; speak clearly and calmly; avoid the use of jargon; keep to an arranged time limit'

■   'Mike's going to have to manage his time better – I want him to make a minimum of 25 sales calls every week'

■   'Louise will have to learn to speak up when she's on the 'phone – I want her to speak clearly, without shouting, so that customers can hear what she is saying and don't have to ask her to repeat everything'.

Once you know what it is you want people to do, then you can give some thought to the coaching technique that will be most effective and most likely to produce the desired results.

ACTIVITY 19

Think back to the coaching you have received during the course of your own career. List three different activities you could use, as a manager, to coach members of staff to enable them to learn new skills, attitudes or knowledge.

1

2

3

FEEDBACK

There are a number of different coaching techniques which can be used in a variety of different situations, with different people:

- **self-directed learning** – asking the learner to research specific information and feed this back to you
- **observation of a demonstration** – asking the learner to observe someone who is modelling expert skills (either yourself or someone else)
- **discussion** – discussing, with the learner, through question and answer and 'general conversation' the skills, knowledge or attitudes you want the learner to acquire
- **specific tasks/special projects** – asking the learner to complete a specific task or special project which involves using particular skills, attitudes or information
- **role-playing specific scenarios** – role-playing, with the learner, a specific scenario (e.g. 'OK, I'm going to negotiate for a 20 per cent discount – show me how you'd handle it') and then reviewing and discussing what happened

- **team/group discussions** – setting up a team meeting to discuss a specific issue with you acting as Chair and tutor, providing constructive comments and feedback on the group's input and suggestions
- **work shadowing** – arranging for the learner to work alongside or observe a more experienced member of staff (either yourself or someone else)
- **special opportunities** – these may include:
  - championing someone so they can attend a special training course
  - putting someone forward for a prestige project team
  - giving someone a chance to attend a special company social event
  - allowing people to meet important suppliers, subcontractors and customers.

CASE STUDY

It's important to use a range of different coaching techniques as Anna, an NHS Trust Manager, explains:

'In a previous job my line manager used to think that coaching was simply a matter of giving me a report to read. "Read that, Anna," he used to say," and then we'll talk about it some time." Well, I soon got wise to that. I didn't read the reports, and he never suggested we discuss them. Fortunately for me, there was a manager in the organization who spotted that I was ambitious and keen to get on. She gave me many opportunities to learn and her coaching took many different forms – she would include me in meetings and special projects, give me complex tasks and assignments, often throw me in at the deep end. But she always took the time to review what I'd done, and to make suggestions for improvement. And no matter what happened, she always supported me – even when I made a real mess of something. She took responsibility for helping me to learn – and that meant a great deal to me.'

Helping learners to learn

When you have your 'Coach's Hat' on, the main skills you will need to use are:

- **Communication** – listening, summarizing, explaining, questioning, using appropriate body language, interpreting body language.
- **Transfer of knowledge and skills** – through explanations, demonstrations, modelling, discussions and de-briefing.
- **Encouragement and support** – through providing positive and useful feedback, praise, recognition of effort and achievement.
- **Review of progress and planning for the future** – through discussion of what has been achieved and what still needs to be achieved, and identification of future learning opportunities.

ACTIVITY 20

Read through the brief case studies that follow and then tick the box which most accurately reflects your chosen response, giving the reason for your response.

Case study 1

Gerry, Administration Manager, approaches Bill, his Senior Administration Clerk and says: 'I'm deeply unhappy with the way you are handling customer 'phone calls. I want you to sit by me and listen to the way I handle customers, because there's got to be an improvement in your attitude.'

How useful is this approach, on a scale of 1 to 5, where 1 is really useful and likely to produce excellent results; and 5 is not at all useful and not at all likely to produce excellent results?

(tick one box only)

1 ❑   2 ❑   3 ❑   4 ❑   5 ❑

Reason for your response

Case study 2

Caroline, Sales Manager, spends over an hour with Jon, one of the sales team, carefully explaining targets and planning learning activities. At the end of the discussion Jon confides that he doesn't think he can meet his targets and he's not at all sure about the training and learning that lie ahead for him.

Caroline says 'Well, targets are targets, and you're going to have to get on with it and meet them – that's what selling is all about. Look, Jon, I don't want to think I've wasted over an hour of my time on this … you need the training, I've booked it and that's all there is to it.'

How useful is this approach, on a scale of 1 to 5, where 1 is really useful and likely to produce excellent results; and 5 is not at all useful and not at all likely to produce excellent results?

(tick one box only)

1 ❑   2 ❑   3 ❑   4 ❑   5 ❑

Reason for your response

Case study 3

Sam, Senior Partner in a law firm, offers to take Susan, a newly qualified solicitor, to a meeting with an important client so that she can gain an insight into the background of a particularly complex case. Susan acknowledges the offer, but says she would really prefer to spend the time looking through the files and then discussing her findings with Sam. He agrees to this.

How useful is this approach, on a scale of 1 to 5, where 1 is really useful and likely to produce excellent results; and 5 is not at all useful and not at all likely to produce excellent results?

(tick one box only)

1 ❑   2 ❑   3 ❑   4 ❑   5 ❑

Reason for your response

Case study 4

Barbara, Director of Human Resources, has been coaching Linda in negotiation skills for some time. Barbara now feels that it's time for Linda to try her wings in a real-life situation. They meet with a supplier to renegotiate a long-standing contract and Linda is in charge of the meeting. Linda achieves the deal she and Barbara had agreed but, when the supplier leaves, Barbara says 'You were really lucky to have got away with that! Why didn't you do what I told you to do? Stick to what I tell you next time!'

How useful is this approach, on a scale of 1 to 5, where 1 is really useful and likely to produce excellent results; and 5 is not at all useful and not at all likely to produce excellent results?

(tick one box only)

1 ❑   2 ❑   3 ❑   4 ❑   5 ❑

Reason for your response

FEEDBACK

Case study 1

This approach is not very useful as Bill is likely to feel demotivated and even resentful. A better approach would be for Gerry to say something like: 'I'm going to be dealing with customer 'phone calls this afternoon and I'd like you to sit in to give me some background on the customers. As a matter of fact, you might find it helpful to listen in, because I've noticed that you've had one or two problems with difficult customers. Hopefully, we can help each other this afternoon.'

Case study 2

This approach is not very useful as it doesn't address the real problems, which are (a) why Jon doesn't think he can meet his targets and (b) why Jon is unsure about the training. A better approach would be for Caroline to say something like: 'I'm really glad that you felt you could mention this to me. What is it about your targets that concerns you most? Is it the quantity of sales, is it the time-frame, or is it something else?'

Case study 3

This is a helpful approach because, although Susan isn't 'doing what Sam wants her to do', she is making a real commitment to learning. It may be that she understands her own learning style, and knows that she will gain more information from reading notes than she would from listening to a conversation. In the circumstances Sam shouldn't feel annoyed because his suggestion has not been accepted. He should recognize that Susan is taking real responsibility for getting to grips with a complex case.

Case study 4

This is not a helpful approach. Linda achieved the desired outcome, in her own way. Barbara's criticism (which is really about her own self-importance, rather than results), is neither useful nor relevant. A much better approach would be to say something like: 'Well done! You handled him really well. What made you decide to go with that approach, rather than the tactics we had agreed?' This would give Linda an opportunity to explain her thinking, at which point Barbara might (a) learn something herself or (b) be able to explain why Linda was fortunate on this occasion but why, on another occasion with a different person, Linda's approach might not work.

The most effective coaches tend also to be the most successful managers. They are people who:

- bring out the best in the individuals they manage
- encourage people to develop skills and abilities by giving them new experiences
- set challenging goals and targets for their people
- are tolerant of genuine mistakes (because they understand the learning cycle)
- provide encouragement, praise and support
- have the courage to take risks and delegate.

Preparing a coaching plan

Once you have identified that there needs to be an improvement in either skills, knowledge or attitude, your next step is to prepare a coaching plan which will enable the learner to close the gap between poor performance and good performance.

ACTIVITY 21

List three key items of information that a coaching plan should contain:

1

2

3

FEEDBACK

Every coaching plan should contain the following key items of information:

- targets – the specific and measurable improvement you hope to achieve in performance, e.g. 'Tim to make a minimum of 25 sales calls each week'
- coaching technique(s) – details of the specific coaching techniques you plan to use in order achieve the targets you have set, e.g. 'discussion and work-shadowing'
- deadline – a specific time target by which the learning should have taken place, e.g. 'target to be achieved by 21 March 2005'
- monitoring and review – an outline of the way in which you intend to monitor and review progress with the learner, e.g. '(a) Check weekly log sheets; (b) Meet with Mike every Monday morning for 3 weeks to discuss progress; (c) Final meeting on 21 March to compare actual performance (log sheets) with target performance'.

ACTIVITY 22

Use this activity to prepare a coaching plan for two different members of staff.

- **Plan 1**
  - Name:

  - Job title:

  - Aspect of performance for improvement:

  - Improvement target:

  - Deadline for improvement:

  - Coaching technique(s):

  - Method of monitoring and reviewing progress:

- **Plan 2**
  - Name:

  - Job title:

  - Aspect of performance for improvement:

  - Improvment target:

  - Deadline for improvement:

  - Coaching technique(s):

  - Method of monitoring and reviewing progress:

Learning summary

- The main aim of coaching is to develop people's work performance by:
  - delegating work that is complex, new, different, challenging or important
  - increasing the level of responsibility that someone assumes
  - providing the right environment and conditions in which someone can learn and practise new skills, knowledge and attitudes.
- In circumstances where specific improvements are required from individual members of staff, coaching targets should be set. Coaching targets should be SMART:
  - **S**imple
  - **M**easurable
  - **A**chievable
  - **R**ealistic
  - **T**ime related.
- Coaching techniques include providing opportunities for:
  - self-directed learning
  - observation of a demonstration by an expert
  - one-to-one discussion
  - team/group discussion
  - specific tasks/special projects
  - role-playing specific scenarios
  - work shadowing.
- A coaching plan should contain the following information:
  - targets
  - coaching techniques to be used
  - deadline for completion
  - method of monitoring and reviewing progress.

Into the workplace

You need to:

- coach team members to develop their skills.

Section 5 Delegating

Introduction

Delegating tasks can be used to develop skills, confidence and commitment. It also has the added advantage that it frees up your time to focus on other things. Opportunities for development are realized at the same time as providing real outcomes in the workplace.

However, delegation isn't the same as simply allocating a task. When you delegate as a developmental opportunity you need to carefully structure the process, giving enough support whilst delegating authority but retaining joint accountability.

How to delegate

For delegation to work, it is important to systematically work through a seven-stage process:

1 Define the task
2 Set targets and standards
3 Choose the right person
4 Fully brief your chosen person
5 Provide the right resources
6 Monitor progress and give feedback
7 Trust and let go!

We look at each of these stages in turn.

1 DEFINE THE TASK

Regardless of the circumstances, your first priority is to clearly define:

- the **task**
- the **standards** to which you want the task completed
- the **time scale** available for completion of the task.

As the person who is delegating, you are the only one who can specify:

- **what** it is you want done
- to what **standard** you want it done
- **when** you want it done by.

It is both unreasonable and unfair to delegate work unless:

(a) you know the precise boundaries and parameters of the work
(b) you pass this information on to the person who will be carrying out the work and shouldering the responsibilities.

It is important to remember that, unless you tell them, people will not know what to do. What is worse, a team member may try to guess and end up making matters even worse. No matter how busy, how stressed or how pressured you are, until you are clear about what it is you want someone to do, the task you are delegating has little chance of success.

ACTIVITY 23

Think back over your own career and recall a time when work was delegated to you but you were unclear about the task, the standards and/or the time frame.

1   How did you feel about the work?

2   How easy or difficult was it for you to carry out the work?

3 Did you complete the work successfully?

4 How did you feel towards the person who delegated the work without giving you sufficient information?

It's likely that if the task was not properly delegated and you were given insufficient information then you may have felt some or all of the following emotions:

- powerlessness
- uncertainty
- irritation
- resentfulness
- indecisiveness
- anxiousness
- depression
- anger
- incompetence.

When people are asked to do something, but are not properly briefed, their motivation and morale will dip as it raises concerns such as:

- will I keep my job?
- will I still be accepted as part of the team?
- will I make a mess of it?
- if I mess it up, will I ever be given any challenging or interesting work again?

2 SET TARGETS AND STANDARDS

Before briefing your chosen person it is important that you give thought to the targets and standards of performance you expect.

Targets and standards can be set using:

- Milestones
- Performance indicators
- Standards of performance.

Milestones

'Milestones' are time-related points which occur at frequent intervals throughout the life of a project and which indicate the time by which a task should be completed. So for a project involving solving a problem, the individual task milestones might look something like those shown below.

Task	Week 1	Week 2	Week 3	Week 4	Week 5
Collect data	███	███			
Analyse data for root cause			███		
Identify possible solution				███	
Prepare and present report					███

ACTIVITY 24

Think back to the last time you delegated work.

1   What criteria did you use to set the task or project milestones? (For example, did you base your milestones on the amount of time it would take you to complete the task? Were the milestones driven by a specific project deadline?)

2   Were all of the milestones achieved or did some parts of the task or project fall behind schedule?

3   What were the reasons for your answer to **(2)** above?

4   When setting task or project milestones in the future, what might you do differently and why?

FEEDBACK

A key activity, when setting milestones, is to make sure that the person who is actually going to be doing the work agrees that the milestones are reasonable and can be achieved. Unless you can get agreement and co-operation, the milestones become meaningless.

CASE STUDY

Rose, MD of a haulage company, explains:

When I was a new and inexperienced manager I delegated a project to someone on my team and I set the milestone without any kind of negotiation or consultation. I had a deadline to meet, the work had to be done and that was that. Ross, the person who was on the receiving end of all this tried to tell me I was asking for the impossible, but I wasn't interested. I thought I could probably do it in the timescale, and I didn't see why he couldn't do it. To cut a long story short Ross, because of the unreasonable time pressures I'd imposed, cut corners to such an extent that we ended up in court. It was a long and costly case and both our reputation and out finances suffered. At the end of the day you have to be realistic and, above all, you have to be prepared to listen to people and be prepared to negotiate and compromise.

Performance indicators

Performance indicators can be set to provide information about what is happening in any task or process. This information will give you feedback on progress and will help you to determine whether you are satisfied or dissatisfied with what is happening.

For example, supposing you decided that you want to improve the quality of customer care which customers receive when they telephone your organization with a query or complaint. You delegate the task of making the improvements to a member of your team. You set the following performance indicators:

- number of calls dealt with by each customer service telephonist
- length of call
- number of customers who are still dissatisfied at the end of conversation with customer service telephonist
- cost to the company of the customer service intervention – refund, replacement, credit note, free carriage, etc.

You provide performance indicator charts for each customer service telephonist and you ask each person to complete a chart every time they finish a call. At the end of the day all of the figures on the charts are collated. Over a period of time it is possible to see, from the performance indicators, whether there is any kind of improvement or deterioration in performance. An example of how this works is shown below.

Week	Average number of daily calls dealt with	Average length of each call (minutes)	Average number of customers still dissatisfied at the end of the call	Average cost to the company of customer service intervention (£)
Week 1				
Mon 4/11	20	20	14	9
Tues 5/11	19	25	12	17
Wed 6/11	28	15	13	12.50
Thurs 7/11	28	15	10	19
Fri 8/11	37	12	7	22
Week 2				
Mon 11/11	49	9	5	23
Tues 12/11	49	9	4	23
Wed 13/11	57	8	4	26
Thurs 14/11	55	8	2	25
Fri 15/11	56	8	1	27

The performance indicators shown above provide the following information:

Week 1 (4/11 to 8/11)

■ The average number of daily calls dealt with increased from 20 to 37.

■ The average length of each call decreased from 20 to 12 minutes.

■ The average number of customers still dissatisfied at the end of each call decreased from 14 to 7.

■ The average cost to the company of each customer service intervention increased from £9 to £22.

Week 2 (11/11 to 15/11)

■ The average number of daily calls dealt with increased from 49 to 56.

■ The average length of each call decreased from 9 to 8 minutes.

■ The average number of customers still dissatisfied at the end of each call decreased from 5 to 1.

■ The average cost to the company of each customer service intervention increased from £23 to £27.

Clearly, over the 2-week period that your team member has been working to improve customer service, there has been:

■ A significant increase in the number of calls dealt with on a daily basis (up from 20 per day to 56 per day over the 2-week period.

■ A significant decrease in the amount of time spent with each individual customer (down from 20 to 8 minutes over the 2-week period).

■ A significant decrease in the number of dissatisfied customers (down from 14 to 1 over the 2-week period).

■ A significant increase in the cost to the company of each customer service intervention (up from £9 to £27).

The performance indicators show more customers being dealt with, with more speed and efficiency, and much less customer dissatisfaction. The down-side is that the improvement in customer service is costing the company more. Whether or not that is acceptable depends on the company, its vision, values and long-term strategy. But the performance indicators let you know:

1   What is happening
2   Whether or not the action is making a positive difference.

Performance indicators can provide information about, amongst other things:

■ Deadlines	■ Budgets
■ Cash flow	■ Sales
■ Delivery	■ Quality
■ Stock levels	■ Patients treated
■ Delays	■ Time taken
■ Money spent	■ Customer complaints
■ Successes	■ Failures

ACTIVITY 25

Part 1

1 Identify a task or project which you intend to delegate in the near future. Note down brief details in the space below.

2 Identify up to five performance indicators which will provide information about the progress of the task or project.

Part 2

(Note: work through this part of the activity after the completion of your delegated task or project.)

1 Whilst your team member was working on the task or project, how frequently did you check the information provided by the performance indicator?

2   Did the information provided by the performance indicators encourage you to change any aspect of the task or project, or your instructions to your team member?

3   Please give your reasons for your response to question (**2**) above.

Standards of performance

It is your responsibility to set the standards of performance that you require. Setting standards is rather like setting objectives, in that both standards and objectives need to be:

- simple
- measurable
- achievable
- realistic.

and may be related to:

- time
- cost
- quantity
- quality.

Some examples of standards of performance:

Task:	Organize a sales conference
Delegate to:	Marjorie King
Start date:	18th March
Deadline:	Conference to be held on 9th May

1 issue all invitations by 1st April
2 book a four-star hotel within 20 mile-radius of Birmingham
3 choose menu for buffet at a cost of not more than £12 per person
4 prepare timetable for 3-hour presentation
5 organize a minimum of four speakers, one from each region
6 draft two-page programme/brochure describing the day's events
7 negotiate deal with printers – brochure: 2 colours, glossy paper, 2 pages, 100 copies.

When delegating, the importance of setting standards cannot be emphasized too much. Imagine what might happen if, instead of defining the performance standards described above, you simply say, 'Book a decent hotel and arrange a buffet. We'll need some speakers … Oh and don't forget we'll need some colour brochures as well.' That kind of delegation is unfair to everyone involved.

3 CHOOSE THE RIGHT PERSON

When delegating for development you need to think about:

- the gap between the team member's current experience and the experience he or she needs to complete the task. Will the task you intend to delegate help to close this gap?
- previous training or development opportunities in which the team member has participated. Will the task you intend to delegate enable your team member to use some of their newly acquired skills or knowledge?
- readiness for additional responsibility. Has the team member demonstrated his or her readiness for more complex, challenging and responsible work? Will the task you intend to delegate provide these extra opportunities?

4 BRIEF YOUR CHOSEN PERSON

When delegating, particularly if you are stressed or harried, there is a real temptation to rush the process. You know what you want … but don't have the time to go into all the details. This is really a dangerous approach.

Make the time and take the time to meet with your team member to explain the details of the project. Make sure you let the team member know that you recognize it is a development opportunity and make it clear you will be available for guidance and consultation if and when that becomes necessary.

Make sure you establish a good two-way communication. Encourage the team member to ask questions and be prepared to answer them honestly and thoroughly. Ask plenty of open questions to encourage the team member to discuss their queries and concerns, but also to show that you respect their expertise and opinion.

Make sure you agree the milestones, performance indicators and standards of performance. Don't impose them. Go through each one and, where necessary, be prepared to negotiate and compromise. Setting someone up for failure is demotivating and demoralizing for everyone concerned.

5 PROVIDE THE RIGHT RESOURCES

It is your responsibility to make sure that your team member has:

- sufficient time
- sufficient and appropriate resources
- sufficient and appropriate authority.

To complete the task successfully, no matter how intelligent or resourceful someone might be, if they don't have the budget or the equipment or the people they need, it is highly unlikely that they will be able to achieve the outcome you want.

You must also delegate sufficient authority to do the job properly and **other people must be informed that the delegate has the authority**.

6 MONITOR PROGRESS AND GIVE FEEDBACK

It is important to monitor progress for two reasons. The first is that delegation is not an abdication of responsibility. The second is that delegates need support, and need to know how they are doing. If things are going well they will appreciate the reward of a few words of praise. If things are going badly your team member will need the opportunity to ask for advice or guidance. Someone may feel reluctant to ring you and say, 'I'm having trouble', but if a date has been set for a progress review, problems can be aired easily and naturally as part of the review process.

7 TRUST AND LET GO!

This is a vital part of the delegation process. The cause of people being frightened to trust is often due to one or more of the following factors. They:

- would really prefer to do the job themselves
- think they could do a better job themselves
- lack confidence in the team member
- are perfectionists who cannot bear people to make mistakes.

It is crucial for success to recognize that there is every chance that things will go wrong. It is important to accept that, if someone else does the job, they will not do it in exactly the same way you would. If your team member knows what they have to do and have the necessary support from you, then you just have to trust and let go. Of course you need to keep a watchful eye on progress and be prepared to step in if necessary, but you must also give your team member the space to get on with the job and develop their skills.

ACTIVITY 26

The next time you use delegation as a development tool, note down details of each stage below.

1 Define the task

2 Setting standards

- What standards for performance did you set?

■ What was the timescale for completion of the task?

3 Choosing the right person

■ What were the specific development needs of the person you selected?

■ What existing skills and knowledge did they bring to the task?

4 Briefing

■ How did you brief your team member?

■ At the end of the briefing, are you completely satisfied that your team member knew exactly what was expected of them? If not, what did you do about it?

5 Providing the right resources

■ How did you determine how much time would be needed?

■ How did you determine what resources would be needed?

■ How did you make sure that your team member had the necessary authority to carry out the task?

6   **Monitoring progress and providing feedback**

  ■   How did you plan to monitor and provide feedback?

7   **Trusting and letting go**

  ■   Did you have any difficulties trusting and letting go? If so, how did you deal with it?

Learning summary

■   Delegation is a very effective means of developing team members to take on more demanding, complex or responsible work.

■   The seven stages of successful delegation are:

  1   Define the task
  2   Set targets and standards
  3   Choose the right person
  4   Fully brief your chosen person
  5   Provide the right resources
  6   Monitor progress and give feedback
  7   Trust and let go.

■   Targets and standards can be set by using:

  –   Milestones
  –   Performance indicators
  –   Standards of performance.

- When delegating for development you need to think about:
  - the gap between the team member's current experience and the experience he or she needs to complete the task
  - previous training or development opportunities in which the team member has participated
  - readiness for additional responsibility.
- Briefing your team member involves making time to explain the task thoroughly and ensure open channels of communication.
- Providing the right resources involves making sure your team member has sufficient and appropriate:
  - time
  - equipment and other tangible resources
  - authority.
- You need to monitor progress, provide feedback and remember to let go.

Into the workplace

You need to:

- use delegation as a method of developing members of your team.

Section 6 Mentoring

Introduction

Many successful people can look back and acknowledge that, in some part, their current success is due to the assistance and support they received from a mentor at some point in their career.

'What does a Mentor actually do?' is the key question. Here are some definitions to give you an insight into the role of the mentor:

Mentoring is a powerful system for making progress. It depends on the positive partnership of two people; a 'junior' partner, the mentee or protégé, who wants to get ahead and a 'senior' partner, the mentor, someone who is already ahead, who wants to help the junior learn the ropes.

Lily Segerman-Peck[1]

To mentor can mean to:

- *befriend, support and counsel;*
- *help an individual towards personal growth;*
- *help a group develop and grow.*

Clare Freeman[2]

A good mentor provides personal/emotional support, personal feedback, emotional and intellectual challenge, and a role model of someone who embodies many of the characteristics and skills that the [learner] seeks to develop.

Margot Cairnes[3]

In this section of the workbook we will be looking at the importance of the mentor/protègè relationship – both for the organization and for the individuals involved – and considering how you could make a positive contribution to the mentoring process within your organization.

The difference between a coach and a mentor

Coaching is usually about moving someone from 'can't do' or 'can't do very well' to 'can do' or 'can do it better now', and often involves the transfer of specific knowledge and skills from one person to another, most often in accordance with an agreed coaching plan. For example:

■ 'I'll do it – you watch – then you copy what I do'
■ 'Have a go at this task and see how you get on'
■ 'Show me how you usually do it – OK – now try it this way'.

Mentoring is a different approach altogether. The mentoring task involves sharing time and wisdom, and giving advice and direction. This process, when undertaken voluntarily and with a generous spirit, can often have a profoundly beneficial effect on others, both professionally and personally.

You have, almost certainly, at some point in your life, looked to a mentor for information, help, advice, encouragement and support. Right now, perhaps without even realizing it, you may be a mentor to a colleague at work. For example, if there is someone at work who:

■ quizzes and questions you about how you might tackle a specific problem, or handle a specific situation
■ gives the impression that they hold you in very high regard and, maybe, even think of you as the 'fount of all knowledge'
■ often refer to your achievements, views or opinions when in conversation with others: 'Well, Sue Taylor thinks that …'

then it could be that they regard you as their informal mentor.

ACTIVITY 27

Consider the mentors you have had during your career to date. List three key tasks that those people have performed for you:

1

2

3

FEEDBACK

Mentors assist their protégés by:

- providing insight – perhaps into the culture of the organization; or into the 'politics' or economics of business life; or into the traditions that surround a particular profession
- providing continuous personal support
- acting as a confidential sounding board for hopes, fears and ambitions
- helping the learner to come to terms with real-life problems, as they occur in the real world by offering the benefit of his or her practical experience
- demonstrating to the learner how, in business, theory relates to practice – 'forget the text books – this is what actually happens'
- acting as a role model.

CASE STUDY

Simon, a garage manager, describes his relationship with a mentor.

'Stan was my first boss – he owned the garage where I was employed as a very, very junior sales assistant. During the time I worked for him he taught me everything I know about cars, selling, life, relationships, money … he was my boss, a good friend, a wonderful teacher and my role model. When he died and the firm closed down I was far more upset about losing Stan than I was about losing the job.'

ACTIVITY 28

Consider the characteristics of a **good** mentor and a **poor** mentor, and then complete the chart below.

Key characteristics of a GOOD mentor	Key characteristics of a POOR mentor
1	1
2	2
3	3
4	4

FEEDBACK

In response to the last activity you probably listed some of the following key characteristics:

Good mentors:

- consistently model the skills, attitudes and abilities to which the protégé aspires
- recognize the importance of personal and professional development, and share their knowledge and experience generously and willingly
- accept, totally, that there is more than one way to do something, and allow people the freedom to achieve the desired results in their own way, using their own methods
- demonstrate flexible attitudes and proactive behaviour – and encourage others to do the same
- provide supportive feedback on potential, abilities, strengths and areas where further development is needed
- offer recognition of effort and achievement.

Poor mentors:

- seek to dominate their protégés and impose their own opinions, solutions, tactics or ideology – 'do as I do, think as I do, and you'll get on all right'
- use the role of mentor to work to their own agenda – for instance, exert undue influence on their protégés to encourage them to act in the best interests of the mentor (or their particular function), rather than the best interests of the protégé or the organization
- 'go through the motions' of being a mentor without any real commitment to the role
- adopt rigid, inflexible attitudes – 'we've always done it like this, and it's always worked before, so there's no reason to change things'
- assume that they are always right and they always know best
- offer judgemental rather than constructive criticism; biased rather than unbiased feedback
- harbour negative feelings – jealousy, bitterness or resentment – because, in their view, the protégé is enjoying benefits (perhaps the advantage of having a mentor) which they didn't have access to when they were climbing the ladder to success
- pay little or no attention to establishing and maintaining a good relationship with their protégé.

Establishing and maintaining a good working relationship

Within a formal mentoring programme, the key to success is the quality of the relationship between the mentor and their protégé. People – whether junior staff starting out on a career path or senior managers who have almost reached the top of the corporate ladder – are often likely to have some reservations about being assigned a mentor.

ACTIVITY 29

For the purpose of this activity imagine that you have been told that a more senior manager has been assigned to you as your mentor, and that you are required to attend an initial meeting with this person to establish the ground rules. Consider the statements below and tick whichever could apply to you.

Prior to the initial meeting with my mentor I might feel:

Yes

- Concerned that my mentor and I might not be able to establish a close working relationship. ❏
- Apprehensive about issues of confidentiality. ❏
- Unwilling to disclose too much too soon. ❏
- Anxious that, perhaps, my mentor might have been 'rail roaded' into taking on this additional role, and so might be an unwilling participant in the programme. ❏
- Worried about the way in which my progress on the mentoring programme might affect my status or career prospects within the company. ❏
- Anxious not to get into a conflict situation with my mentor. ❏
- Concerned that my mentor might interfere in the way I do my job. ❏
- Unwilling to reveal too many personal details. ❏

FEEDBACK

Your responses to this activity will, of course, be personal to you. However, most people who approach their first meeting their mentor are likely to experience many, if not all, of these concerns.

CASE STUDY

Paul, a senior manager in merchant banking, explains how he felt when he was informed that he had been selected for inclusion in his company's mentoring programme.

'Quite soon after I joined this company I was told that the Vice-President was to be my mentor. I didn't know Steve at the time – from where I was standing he seemed to be a high-flying whiz-kid from New York and I couldn't see how we would be able to relate to one another, let alone work together in a fairly intimate relationship. In addition, I felt disadvantaged because he held such a senior position and, it seemed to me, that I'd be firmly in the spotlight and under the microscope. That didn't appeal to me at all. In the event, it actually worked very well and I learned a great deal from him. So much so that I applied for, and got, a job with the company at the head office in Boston. I was able to make the transition from working here at home in the UK to working in the US because I learned so much from Steve – both about our company and about the American way of doing business. So, a situation I initially perceived as potentially quite dangerous in fact turned out to be a golden opportunity.'

Mentors, too, sometimes feel as though they may have bitten off more than they can chew by volunteering to participate in the programme.

ACTIVITY 30

1   Take a few minutes to identify any concerns you personally might have if you were asked to take on the role of mentor to someone in your organization. Note your ideas below.

Concerns I would have about taking on the role of mentor:

2   Now think about the benefits of undertaking this role within your organization.

Benefits I might enjoy as a result of taking on the role of mentor:

FEEDBACK

Common **concerns** that mentors have before the mentoring process begins include:

- Is this going to take up too much of my time?
- How is this going to impact on my job performance?
- Is this person going to expect too much from me, in terms of time and energy?
- I'm not the right kind of person to be agony aunt, counsellor and problem solver!

If you do decide to act as a mentor (and this always works best when the mentors volunteer their services), make sure that you set clear boundaries for the relationship. You can do this by being clear about:

- the amount of time, each week, you are prepared to devote to the task of being a mentor
- what level of personal involvement will be comfortable for you. For example:
  - would you be prepared to spend personal time with your protégé? Perhaps going for a drink or a meal after work, or visiting the gym or the golf-club together?
  - would you be happy for your protégé to have your home number so that they could call you in the evening or at the weekends?
  - as the relationship progresses, where would want you to draw the line with regard to the discussion of personal topics – finance? relationships? religion? politics?
  - would you feel more or less comfortable with a protégé of the opposite sex? If so, why? In what way would this impact on the mentoring relationship?
  - what practical steps can you to take to make sure that your own role and responsibilities are not adversely affected by the additional tasks involved in the mentoring process?

Only you know the answers to these questions, and it is important that you address these issues before the mentoring programme gets under way.

Benefits to mentors include:

- having an opportunity to make a valuable contribution to your organization by helping to develop someone's potential
- increased personal self-confidence and self-esteem
- increased sense of personal achievement and job satisfaction
- opportunity to enhance your own existing skills, or develop new ones
- higher profile within your organization
- access to new people, sources of information, resources
- enhanced prospects for promotion or career development.

Setting up a mentoring programme

Organizations run many different kinds of mentoring programmes, including:

- programmes for a specific group of people:
    - junior, middle or senior managers
    - women, ethnic or other minority groups
    - new recruits to the company
    - staff who are actively seeking career progression
    - teams who are about to undertake new projects.
- programmes for specific purposes:
    - develop staff to enable them to step into more senior roles
    - support staff at times when the organization is undergoing rapid or complex change
    - introduce self-managed learning
    - enable people to develop new and complex skills, e.g. European languages; working with advanced technology; undertaking negotiations in S.E. Asia
    - support managers who are undertaking specific kinds of training or learning activities, e.g. MBA by distance learning; NVQ level 4/5; NVQ Assessor Programme; part-time MA or MSc at a local university.

CHOOSING THE MENTORS

In most organizations that run mentoring programmes, the mentors are chosen from volunteers at middle and senior management levels.

Mentors should be able to offer participants in the programme:

- in-depth knowledge and understanding of the business, profession or specialism in which the protégé is engaged (e.g. public relations, health care, architecture) plus a clear insight into the culture and workings of the company for which both mentor and protégé work
- a sincere belief that mentoring is a worthwhile and beneficial process for everyone involved
- good communication skills
- willingness to create rapport and establish a good working relationship
- ability to motivate and inspire
- respect, honesty, integrity, confidentiality and a commitment to ethical behaviour in all dealings between the mentor and the protégé.

Training the mentors

It really isn't sufficient to identify suitable mentors and then simply expect they will carry out the role. Anyone who is going to undertake the role of mentor should have some initial training and preparation so that they can carry out their role professionally, and to the very best of their ability.

ACTIVITY 31

For the purpose of this activity, imagine that you have been asked to create a one- or two-day training programme for the people who are going to act as mentors within your organization. List five topics you would present during the training:

1

2

3

4

5

FEEDBACK

All of the following topics could usefully be included in a mentors' training programme:

- what mentoring is, and what it is not
- the benefits of mentoring for the organization, and for everyone involved
- the role of the mentor
- mentor skills
- the qualities which a good mentor should possess, and the behaviours which should be avoided
- potential pitfalls and problems, and how to overcome them
- how long the mentoring process/relationship is likely to last
- ways in which the mentors can access guidance, support and encouragement for themselves (if the going gets tough).

Organizing the programme

A mentoring programme can be organized in a variety of different ways, including any combination of the following:

- one-to-one meetings between mentor and protégé
- core group meetings attended by the protégés who are, maybe, at the same managerial level, or from the same department, function or unit, plus their mentors
- whole group meetings between all the protégés on the programme, plus all the mentors
- one-day training sessions
- weekend residential sessions
- informal 'get-togethers'.

In addition, protégés' line managers (those who are not involved as mentors) may also be invited to attend some of the meetings as this helps to involve them, and keeps the lines of communication open.

Use the next activity to identify the strategy you might use to create and implement a mentoring programme within your organization.

ACTIVITY 32

Complete the chart below with information relevant to your organization.

Within your current organization ...	
Which group of people would most benefit from being involved as protégés on a mentoring programme?	■
Should the mentoring programme be undertaken with a specific objective in mind? If so, what should that objective be?	■
What method should be used to motivate people to volunteer as mentors?	■
What kind of selection process should be used to select mentors from the volunteer group?	■
Who should be responsible for making the selections?	■
Which person – or group of people – should be responsible for driving the mentoring programme through the organization?	■
How, when and where should mentor training take place?	■
Who should be responsible for mentor training?	■
Who should be responsible for selecting the protégés?	■
How, when and where should the protégés be introduced and inducted into the programme?	■
Who should be responsible for protégé introduction and induction?	■
What system should be used for monitoring success?	■
Who should be responsible for monitoring success?	■
How long should the programme last?	■
What could your personal contribution be to the success of the programme?	■

Learning summary

- Within most organizations the main purposes of mentoring programmes are to:
  - develop managers for more senior roles
  - introduce and support management of change
  - introduce self-managed learning
  - help to develop new or different skills
  - help personal and professional development
  - support managers undertaking education or training.
- The mentoring task involves willingly:
  - sharing time and wisdom
  - providing guidance, advice, encouragement and support
  - helping people to achieve their full potential and climb the ladder to success.
- Mentors can be of most assistance to their protégés by providing:
  - an insight into the profession, the business, the culture
  - continuous personal support
  - a non-critical, non-judgemental listening ear
  - practical links between theory and practice
  - the benefit of his/her experience to solve real-life problems.
- Setting up a mentoring programme involves:
  - deciding which staff will participate as protégés
  - deciding the purpose of the programme
  - choosing the mentors who (ideally) should be given the opportunity to volunteer
  - training the mentors
  - introducing the protégés to the programme
  - deciding on the format of meetings
  - monitoring progress.

Into the workplace

You need to:

- recognize the benefits and practicalities of introducing a mentoring programme into an organization.

References

1   Segerman-Peck, L. (1991) *Networking and Mentoring: A Woman's Guide.* Piatkus

2   Freeman, C. (1994) Mentoring is for personal growth. *Organisations and People* 1(4) (pp. 32–35)

3   Cairnes, M. (1995) Mentoring for success. In *The Practising Manager* 15(2) (pp. 11–16)

Information toolbox

General

Armstrong, M. (1994) *A Handbook of Personnel Management Practice*, Fourth Edn, Kogan Page

Harrison, R. (1998) *Training and Development*, Institute of Personnel Management

Taylor, D. & Bishop, S. (1994) *Readymade Activities for Developing Your Staff*, Institute of Management/Pitman Publishing

Honey, P. (1996) *101 Ways to Develop Your People, Without Really Trying!*, Peter Honey Publications

www.peterhoney.co.uk   Gives access to learning styles questionnaires as well as range of resources related to people development generally

www.belbin.com   Gives access to Team Roles questionnaires

Pedler, M., Burgoyne, J. & Boydell, T. (1997) *The Learning Company*, McGraw-Hill

Planning and delivering training

Peel, M. (1994) *Successful Training in a Week*, Institute of Management, Hodder & Stoughton

Kroehnert, G. (1995) *Basic Training for Trainers*, McGraw-Hill

Coaching

McLeod, A. (2003) *Performance Coaching: The Handbook for Managers, HR professionals and Coaches*, Crown House Publishing

Thorpe, S. & Clifford, J. (2003) *The Coaching Handbook: An Action Kit for Trainers and Managers*, Kogan Page

Mentoring

Carter, S. & Lewis, G. (1994) *Successful Mentoring in a Week*, Institute of Management, Hodder & Stoughton

Norton, B. & Tivey, J. (1995) *Management Directions – Mentoring*, Institute of Management

Investors in People

Investors in People (Iip) is the national Standard which sets out a level of good practice for training and development of people to achieve business goals. Web site contains a lot of useful information and links.

www.iipuk.co.uk